Tahiti Islands travel guide

Tourism, Holiday and Vacation, best destination for self-relaxation

Author
Ade Pearson

Copyright Notice

Copyright © 2017 Global Print Digital
All Rights Reserved

Digital Management Copyright Notice. This Title is not in public domain, it is copyrighted to the original author, and being published by **Global Print Digital**. No other means of reproducing this title is accepted, and none of its content is editable, neither right to commercialize it is accepted, except with the consent of the author or authorized distributor. You must purchase this Title from a vendor who's right is given to sell it, other sources of purchase are not accepted, and accountable for an action against. We are happy that you understood, and being guided by these terms as you proceed. Thank you

First Printing: 2017.

ISBN: 978-1-912483-17-4

Publisher: Global Print Digital.
Arlington Row, Bibury, Cirencester GL7 5ND
Gloucester
United Kingdom.
Website: www.homeworkoffer.com

Table of Content

Touristic Introduction 1
History 4
Culture 24
   Mana 24
   Tattoos 26
   Music and Dance 32
   Crafts 36
   Festivals & Events 37
   Religion 56
Travel and Tourism 58
   Attraction and Activities 59
      Diving & Snorkeling 59
         Marine Environment 60
         Marine Life 62
         Diving 67
         The Other Aquatic Activities 68
      Outdoors 69
      Romance 74
      Cruising & Sailing 75
         Cruises 76
         Yacht Charter 79
         Sailing in the islands 81
         Stopovers 83
         Superyacht Charter 84
      Spas 86
      Golf 90
      Shopping 92
      Traditional Cuisine 96
   The Islands of Tahiti 101
      Tuamotu Islands 101
         Tikehau 101
         Manihi 103
         Rangiroa 104
         Fakarava 106
         Other Tuamotu Islands 108
      Society Islands 112
         Tahiti 113
         Moorea 115

- Raiatea 116
- Bora Bora 118
- Maupiti 120
- Tetiaroa 122
- Huahine 124
- Taha'a 126
- Tupai 128
- Gambier Islands 128
  - Mangareva 129
- Marquesas Islands 130
- Austral Islands 137

Plan your Trip Before you go 142
- Transportation 142
  - Island Hopping 144
  - Airlines 146
  - Cruise Ships 149
- Visas & Entries 154
- Tahitian Customs 158
- Weather 161
- Tahiti Currency 162
- Health in Tahiti 164

Touristic Introduction

Maeva! Welcome!
Tahiti Moorea Bora Bora island names that evoke a wonderful state of mind, seducing honeymooners, romantics, adventurers, and vacationers looking for escape.

Here, around these South Seas isles, a romantic sunset sea sends giant curls of turquoise breaking onto the colorful reefs that protect the tranquil lagoons of warm, bright-emerald waters and white coral-sand beaches.

Tahiti covers over two million square miles of the South Pacific Ocean and is comprised of 118 islands spread over five great archipelagos.

Many islands are crowned with jagged peaks while others appear to barely float above the breaking waves. Spread over an area as large as Western Europe, the total land mass of all the islands adds up to an area only slightly larger than the tiny state of Rhode Island.

The three archipelagos most sought by visitors are the Society Islands, comprised of Tahiti, Moorea, Bora Bora, Huahine, Raiatea and Taha'a; The Tuamotu Atolls or "Tahiti's Strand of Pearls", include the atolls of Rangiroa, Manihi, Tikehau, and Fakarava; and the Marquesas, or "The Mysterious Islands."

The two other archipelagos, the Austral Islands and the Gambier Islands, lie to the south and the southeast, respectively, of the Society Islands. While very few travelers venture to these remote islands, those that do are not disappointed by the pristine environment.

Closer Than You Think

Easier to travel to than you might imagine, Tahiti's Faa'a Airport is under 8 hours by air from Los Angeles LAX airport, with daily nonstop flights. As far south of the equator as Hawaii is north, Tahiti is halfway between California and Australia, on the same side of the International Date Line as North America, and in the same time zone as Hawaii - (only three hours behind California April-October and two hours behind California November-March).

What makes Tahiti so unique for visitors?

People: Embrace the warmth of your Polynesian hosts whose love for their islands is seen through music, dance, and flowers.

Overwater Bungalows: Enjoy the drama and comfort of the world's perfect hotel room while sleeping above soothing lagoon waters.

Cruising: Voyage within the legendary South Pacific aboard luxurious cruise ships, super yachts, or passenger freighter that travel between Tahiti's most beautiful islands.

Polynesian Spas: Experience true relaxation and rejuvenation at one of the many luxurious Polynesian spas while nurtured by the tropical ambience.

Snorkeling & Diving: Share the warm, crystal-clear lagoons and swift ocean passes with schools of impossibly-colored fish, docile sharks, and giant manta rays.

Honeymoons & Romance: Celebrate a new romance or a special anniversary in the most romantic spot on earth. Discover how the seclusion and setting of these islands create one of the world's most desirable honeymoon destinations.

History

About Tahitian History

The era of European exploration began in the 1500s when "ships without outriggers" began to arrive. In 1521, Magellan spotted the atoll of Pukapuka in what is now the Tuamotu Islands and, in 1595, the Spanish explorer Mendaña visited visited the island of Fatu Hiva in the Marquesas. More than 170 years later, Samuel Wallis, captain of the English frigate HMS Dolphin, was the first to visit the island of Tahiti during his journey to discover Terra Australis Incognita, a mythical landmass below the equator thought to balance the northern hemisphere. Wallis named Tahiti "King George III Island" and claimed it for England. Soon after, and unaware of Wallis' arrival, French navigator Louis-Antoine de Bougainville landed on the opposite side of Tahiti and claimed it for the King of France.

European fascination with the islands peaked as news spread of both the mutiny of Captain William Bligh's crew aboard the *HMS Bounty*, and the tales told of the beauty and grace of the Tahitian people. Fascination with Tahiti and the South Pacific continued to expand with the illustrations of Tahitian flora and fauna and the first map of the islands of the Pacific that Captain James Cook brought back. In the 1800s, the arrival of whalers, British missionaries and French military expeditions forever changed the way of life on Tahiti, while also serving to provoke a French-British rivalry for control of the islands.

The Pomare Dynasty ruled Tahiti until 1880 when King Pomare V was persuaded to cede Tahiti and most of its dependencies to France. By 1958, all *The Islands of Tahiti* were reconstituted as an French Overseas Territory and renamed French Polynesia. In 2004, French Polynesia became an Overseas Country within the French Republic with self-governing powers and a mission to provide for her people through commerce and investment.

Our Rich Heritage

Polynesian culture has its roots deep in the mythical origins of great ancestral seafarers who settled in the islands 3,000 years ago..

Our culture was passed on from generation to generation by the sacred word. The oral tradition sustained our culture through the centuries. At times, our stories seemed to be on the verge of extinction, only to rise up again at the last moment. In this centuries-old tradition, today's singers chant the magnificent accents of songs sacred or secular losing their echoes in the constant murmurs of the ocean over the coral reef. It is in this tradition that dancers find inspiration for their extravagant choreography. This tradition also inspires enthusiasts of *va'a* (traditional outrigger canoe) to discover the art of building and sailing their fine outrigger canoes over the ocean and lagoons.

From tradition comes the art of audible percussion from the big, deep *pahu* and the rattling *to'ere*, the art of beautiful, complex tattoos, as well as the art of wood sculpture of the Marquesas. Offspring of the great tiki, these stone statues are still standing among the lava of the *marae* in the bottom of the secret valleys.

In the bountiful Polynesian Islands, all talents converge with natural splendors to make craftsmanship into an art form

The Art of Living - Polynesian Style

"'IA ORA NA," "MAEVA" and "MANAVA"… are three words of greeting with which Polynesians will welcome you.

Proud of their islands, the Polynesians are happy to share their natural *joie de vivre* (joy of living) with their guests. It is a joy expressed in dance and music of all kinds; polyphonic chants from a religious, sacred music group along with the rhythm of percussion from traditional instruments, the *pahu* and *toere*. There may even be harmonies from guitars or ukulele that liven up local orchestras. It is a joy that Polynesians express through their leisure and indulging in their favorite pastimes such as fishing, surfing and traditional outrigger sailing, or through va'a, the emblematic sport of the archipelagos.

Testimonials from the Past

The beauty of *The Islands of Tahiti* and its people have long captivated visitors to our shore.

Bougainville (1768): 'The character of the nation appeared to us as gentle and kindly. It appears that there has never been a civil war on the island nor any specific hatred of any sort although the country is divided into small villages, each with an independent lord; we are convinced that the Tahitians bear good faith to each other and that they never question this. Whether they are in their homes or not, the houses are open day and night. Each person harvests fruit from the first tree they find, takes it into the house and goes in. It appears that for the necessities of life, there is no ownership and everything belongs to everyone.'

James Morrison, second boatswain on board the HMAV 'Bounty' (1789): 'The young women wear their hair long, falling in waves down to their waists and decorated with the white leaves (*hinano*) of the *fara* (pandanus or screw pine) as well as with scented flowers. They also make necklaces with *fara* seeds and flowers that are beautifully arranged. This is not only very flattering but is a bouquet pleasing to themselves as well as to all who are seated near them. All in all these are the most beautiful women that we have seen in these seas...

Customs and Traditions

Cradle of the *Ma'ohi* civilization, stretching into the Polynesian Triangle, the Marquesas Islands have preserved impressive parts of customs and lively traditions. The Tiki, stone statues and the *me'ae* and *paepae*, religious sites and sacred places comprised of raised stones that are aligned in pyramidal structures, can be found on all the islands.

The renaissance of traditional art can be seen in the development of the art of tattooing, the first ancestral expression of politico-social-religious values. Today, it is a decoration and ornament for the body, where the aesthetics of the motifs reflect their original meanings.

It is found again in the renewed expression in dance and polyphonic chants such as the *tarava, ute* or *ru'au* that truly express the depths of the soul of the Polynesian people.

This intense, cultural movement is expressed fully through numerous festive manifestations of which the main one is the grandiose festival of *Heiva i Tahiti* in July, where groups of singers, dancers, musicians and actors up to 150 in all compete in a musical, choreographic and costume extravaganza. Poetry regains its former excellence in the arts of oratory or *'orero* with its spectacular rantings. It is an ancient oral tradition that is often accompanied by the pure sound of the *vivo* or the nasal flute.

The Birthplace of the Overwater Bungalow

The overwater bungalow. This vision of romance was invented in *The Islands of Tahiti* in 1967, and has become the quintessential symbol of this South Pacific paradise, and of mutiny-inspiring experiences. Staying in an overwater bungalow is a "can't miss experience." When you stay in an overwater bungalow, you get direct access to the renowned Tahitian blue lagoons from a private deck along with all the amenities and service of a first class hotel. The overwater bungalow is the pinnacle of the ultimate private getaway.

The overwater bungalow was first conceived and built by three American hotel owners known as "The Bali Hai Boys." They took the traditional local Polynesian grass huts and set them on concrete stilts over the water's edge. Today, most resorts throughout *The Islands of Tahiti* feature luxurious bungalows, suites and villas perched over calm and mesmerizing lagoons.

Tahiti-Inspired Artists

Throughout the history of *The Islands of Tahiti*, many authors, singers, artists, poets and yachtsmen have spent time here. Some of them even died in Tahiti.

These men and women are part of Polynesia's historic heritage, with many of them leaving traces of and testimonies to their island life. They were struck by our islands' charm, hospitality and lifestyle. In their own way, each of them helped promote the fame of our islands worldwide.

➢ Herman Melville (1819-1891), the American author and adventurer, was the first to use the South Seas as a setting for a literary narrative ("Typee," 1846 and "Omoo," 1847). He spent a few months in Tahiti in 1841 arriving on board an Australian whaler and later spent some time on Moorea.

➢ Paul Gauguin (1848-1903), the French painter, began living in Tahiti in 1891 and later moved to the island of Hiva Oa in the Marquesas, where he lived out the last two years of his life. He experienced many misadventures in Tahiti while trying to escape civilization. Gauguin was not always well regarded by the Polynesians especially the Marquesans. However, he remains one of the most influential painters of his century. He is buried in

Atuona Cemetery, Hiva Oa. The Paul Gauguin Museum in Pape'ete (Tahiti) and the Paul Gauguin Cultural Centre in Hiva Oa provide an outline of the life of this nonconformist, as well as reproductions of some of his works.

- Pierre Loti (1850-1923), the French naval officer and author, penned an autobiographical novel in 1879 with our islands as the setting titled, "Rarahu, a Polynesian Idyll," also known as "Le Mariage de Loti." You can swim in the Bain Loti next to a statue of the author erected in 1931.

- Robert Louis Stevenson (1850-1894), the Scottish novelist, visited our islands aboard his yacht, Cosco, during his journey to the Pacific in 1888. He later wrote "In the South Seas" in 1891.

- James Norman Hall (1887-1951), the American author, who wrote "Mutiny on the Bounty" and "The Hurricane" (adapted for the screen) with co-author Charles Nordhoff, made Tahiti his home in the 1920s. He died in 1951 and is buried in Arue on the hillside above his home alongside his Polynesian spouse, Lala, who died in 1985. You can visit the home in which he lived, now converted to a museum and classified as an historic monument: James Norman Hall House in Arue.

- Rupert Brooke (1887-1915), the English poet, who wrote the famous poem, "Manea" in 1914 after visiting Tahiti. This classic poem helped carve out a place for Tahiti in modern English literature.

- Alain Gerbault (1893-1941), the aviator, WWI hero, tennis champion and solo yachtsman (he was the first Frenchman to complete an around-the-world journey by sailing boat), lived for six months in Bora Bora in 1932. He returned in 1940. A fierce defender of Polynesia, he wrote eight books condemning colonialism and the destruction the island paradise. In 1941, Gerbault died of malaria in Timor. In 1947, his remains were returned to the main square of Vaitape in Bora Bora where a commemorative plaque was erected in 1951.

- Marlon Brando (1924-2004), the American actor and director, purchased Tetiaroa after completing the filming of "Mutiny on the Bounty" in 1961. He married his co-star, Tahitian Tarita Teriipaia, with whom he lived for 10 years until 1972.

- Bernard Moitessier (1925-1994), the French yachtsman and author, lived for a dozen years in Tahiti and the Tuamotu Islands. Moitessier moved to the atoll of Ahe, where, together with his wife and son, he devoted himself to cultivating organic fruit and vegetables. He was also a strident critic of nuclear testing in the Pacific.

- Jacques Brel (1929-1978), the Belgian singer-songwriter and actor, retired with his partner to the Marquesas at the end of a successful career aboard his sailing yacht, Askoy. Stricken with lung cancer, Brel lived out the last three years of his life on Hiva Oa. Using his private aircraft, Jojo, Brel provided many services to the islanders. He is buried in Atuona Cemetery. The small Jacques Brel Cultural Centre on Hiva Oa recounts the singer's life in the Marquesas. His song, "Les Marquises," describes the simple lifestyle and strength of the inhabitants of "The Land of Men."

- Joe Dassin (1938-1980), the American-born French singer-songwriter, died in Tahiti. He lived in Tahaa, where he bought a luxurious villa on the beach between Toretorea Point and Tiamahana (accessible only by boat or on foot). A plaque at Le Retro, a restaurant/bar in Pape'ete, commemorates his death on August 20, 1980 following a heart attack.

- Alain Colas (1943-1978), the French yachtsman, was the first to complete a solitary round-the-world race in a multihull. He was lost at sea in 1978 during the Route du Rhum yacht race after having passed the Azores. He began living in Tahiti in the 1970s, where he met a Polynesian, Teura Krause, with whom he had three children.

- Bobby Holcomb (1947-1991), the poet, singer, musician, dancer and painter, moved to Huahine in 1976. He died 14 years later. Holcomb was heavily involved in the Maóhi cultural revival movement alongside other celebrities and artists such as Henri Hiro and John Mairai and is one of the best-known artists in The Islands of Tahiti. He is buried at the foot of the sacred mountain, Mou'a Tapu, in Huahine

The Islands of Tahiti on Film

Our natural scenery has inspired major directors and producers. Feature films show in Polynesia are primarily adaptations of books originally published in English.

Here are a few of the most famous films shot in our islands. Film buffs can seek out filming locations during their trip to *The Islands of Tahiti*.

- **"A Ballad of the South Seas" (1912)** was filmed in Papara by the brother of Georges Méliès. Unfortunately, copies this film can no longer be found.

- **"White Shadows in the South Seas" (1927)**, a co-venture in which Robert Flaherty played a role, was shot in the Marquesas.

Considered to be a crowning achievement in exotic film, this film, co-directed by W.S. "Woody" Van Dyke, Jr. (who also directed "Trader Horn," "Eskimo," the first "Tarzan" films, "San Francisco" and a host of other films), is a very poetic silent film. Admired at the time by the Surrealists, he spoke out against the colonization of the islands of Polynesia, considered a paradise lost.

➢ **"Tapu / Tabu / A story of the South Seas" (1929)**, a silent film by the famous German film director, F. W. Murnau, and based on a story by Robert Flaherty dealing with the daily lives of the islanders, was filmed in Bora Bora. A few scenes showing naked swimmers were censored in the United States and in Finland. The film shoot, which lasted eighteen months, was turbulent and shrouded by legend (because of drownings, poisonings and mysterious explosions supposedly caused by magic spells). Murnau and his team were said to have violated several local taboos by setting up their headquarters in an old burial ground and by filming in sacred reefs. To top it off, Murnau died in a car accident eight days before the film premiered in New York.

➢ **"Last of the Pagans" (1935)**, was directed by Richard Thorpe, a former actor turned director, based on the Melville novel, "Typee," and released by Metro Goldwyn Meyer. The film tells the story of two raids aiming to capture humans: the first raid is carried out by a clan from a neighboring island to take wives by force so they can replenish their "stock" and the second is carried out by whites seeking laborers for phosphate mines. The dialogue is in Tahitian with subtitles.

➢ **"Mutiny on the Bounty."** The first Hollywood version, filmed in 1935, was directed by Frank Lloyd and starred Clark Gable. It played fast and loose with the facts. The better-known 1962 film, shot in 1960/1961 with more than 2,000 actors, 8,000 extras and a budget of $27 million, was a boom to the Polynesian economy. After the shoot, Marlon Brando bought Tetiaroa Atoll. In 1984, a scaled-down version, filmed in Moorea, was released starring Mel Gibson and Anthony Hopkins and directed by Roger Donaldson. Although the *HMS Bounty* was just one of many ships sailing the South Pacific in the 18th century, her mutinous voyage helped make *Otaheite* (or Tahiti, as it is called now) the world's most infamous paradise. The drama and beauty of the islands and her people were showcased in the 1932 book "Mutiny on the Bounty" and the movie adaptations of 1933, 1935 (Best Picture), 1962 (Best Picture nominee), and 1984.

- **"Tahiti ou la Joie de Vivre" (1957)** was a comedy directed by Bernard Borderie starring Georges de Caunes. A reporter asks to be sent to Tahiti to find heaven on earth.

- **"The Restless and the Damned" (1961)**, directed by Yves Allégret. The film tells the story of the troubles of a couple who move to Polynesia to seek their fortune in phosphate mining.

- **"Tiara Tahiti" (1962)** is a British film directed by Ted Kotcheff. An adventurer living in Tahiti unexpectedly runs into his former commanding officer who had him court-martialled. To get even, he decides to make life tough for his adversary, who now works in the tourism business.

- **"Tendre Voyou" (1966)**, directed by Jean Becker starring Jean-Paul Belmondo, relates the escapades of a gigolo.

- **"Hurricane" (1979)**, inspired by the novel by James Norman Hall and Charles Nordoff, was filmed in Bora Bora and directed by Dino de Laurentis. It is a remake of the 1937 film of the same name directed by John Ford.

- **"Le Bourreau des Cœur" (1983)**, directed by Christian Gion, was shot on Tetiaroa and stars Aldo Maccione. The film was a huge success at the box office in France (more than 1.6 million tickets were sold).

- **"Les Faussaires" (1994)**, based on a novel by Romain Gary, "La Tête Coupable," was directed by Frédéric Blum. The protagonist is an author who has come to Tahiti to write a biography on Paul Gauguin.

- **"Love Affair" (1994)**, released by Gaumont, is a love story and a remake of the 1939 film of the same name. It was shot in Tahiti and starred Katharine Hepburn in her last appearance in a film.

- **"Les Perles du Pacifique" (1999)** is a 13-episode television series produced by Gaumont about life on a pearl farm.

- **"Le Prince du Pacifique,"** directed by Alain Corneau and shot in Huahine in 2000, stars Thierry Lhermitte and Patrick Timsit.

- **"South Pacific" (2001)**, a musical comedy directed by Richard Pierce, stars Harry Connick Jr. and Glenn Close.

- **"Couples Retreat"** was released by Universal Studios and shot in Bora Bora in October 2008. With only $7 million invested in the film locally, it was the highest grossing film for Universal that year. Nearly fifty journalists were invited to travel to the filming location by the producers.

- **"L'ordre et la Morale"** directed by Matthieu Kassowitz, was shot in 2010 on Anaa, a small island in the Tuamotu Islands selected as the setting for events in Ouvea (New Caledonia). Events depicted as taking place in Noumea were filmed in Pape'ete.

Other TV shows and documentaries

Every year, the islands are selected as the location for a number of documentaries, TV reality shows, cooking shows and commercials for major international brands. Surfing the waves in Teahupo'o as well as in a few secret spots in the more distant archipelagos is obviously a favorite subject for film. The same can be said of our sharks and whales (which ply our waters from July to November). The US TV series, "Survivor," shot in 2002 in the Marquesas (Nuku Hiva), helped publicize the archipelago in North America.

The Institute for Audiovisual Communication (ICA) is the audiovisual repository for *The Islands of Tahiti*.

For the last 10 years, the Oceania International Documentary Film Festival (FIFO) has been screening the best documentaries on the region. FIFO takes place in February each year at the Maison de la Culture.

Great Outrigger Canoes

The now generally-accepted theory is that it was from south-east Asia that great migrations took place three to four thousand years ago, leading to the settlement of the Pacific by Polynesian populations.

Using outrigger canoes with double sails, built out of wood and plaited fibers, these first intrepid navigators, thanks to their knowledge of the wind, currents and stars were able to travel towards the East, colonizing the archipelagos of the Central Pacific (Cook Islands, *The Islands of Tahiti*...) between 500 BC and 500 AD.

These great expeditions, that ended in about 1000 AD brought about what is known as the "Polynesian Triangle" that is made up of Hawaii (in the north), Easter Island (in the East) and *The Islands of Tahiti* (to the west) and of New Zealand (in the southwest). The different languages used in these islands, that stem from the *Ma'ohi* language, are evidence of the common origin of their inhabitants.

Canoes

Aboard massive, double-hulled outrigger canoes called *tipairua*, Polynesians navigated the vast ocean by stars, winds, and currents and created new civilizations in their wake. Today, the canoe continues to play an important role in everyday Tahitian life and is honored in colorful races and festivals. Centuries before Europeans concluded that the Earth was round, Polynesians had mastered the vast blue expanse of the Pacific.

Hawaiki Nui Va'a: It is the world's largest and longest international open-ocean outrigger canoe race and covers a grueling 77 miles. The race encompasses 3 steps: the 1st one links Huahine to Raiatea, the 2nd one links Raiatea to Taha'a and the last one links Taha'a to Bora Bora. The start and finish are celebrated with a grand festival of tahitian food and music.

The Arrival of the Europeans

In the 16th century, Magellan, then Mendana respectively, reached the Tuamotu and Marquesas Islands. However, it was the Englishman, Samuel Wallis who is memorable in the European discovery of Tahiti (1767). The following year, the Frenchman Antoine de Bougainville baptised this island, "New Cythera." A year later, *The Islands of Tahiti* were divided into several chiefdoms and kingdoms where the Polynesian cosmogony had different divinities. Little by little, Protestant and Catholic missionaries preached the gospel in the islands, and then in 1797, with the help of the Europeans, the chiefs succeeded in establishing their supremacy and created the "Pomare dynasty."

In the nineteenth century, *The Islands of Tahiti* were the scene of Franco-British rivalry that was religious, commercial and strategic at the same time. In 1842, the French Protectorate was finally signed by Queen Pomare IV (on Tahiti and Moorea) then Annexation was accepted in 1880 by Pomare V, last King of Tahiti.

The 1960s marked a turning point for *The Islands of Tahiti* that rushed the region into modern times. With the establishment of the CEP (Pacific Experimentation Centre) in 1963, there was an influx of inhabitants to Tahiti, bringing rapid growth to the local economy.

Chronology of The Islands of Tahiti's History

- From 3,000 to 4,000 BC: the waves of settlers in the south Pacific that came from South-East Asia.
- III VI century: first human settlements in the Marquesas.
- From 850 1000: colonization of the Windward Islands, Hawaii, the Cook Islands, Easter Island and New Zealand from Marquesas.
- 1521: Magellan discovers a part of Tuamotu.
- 1595: Alvero de Mendena discovers the Marquesas.
- 1767: Wallis arrives at Tahiti.
- 1768: Bougainville baptizes this island New Cythera.
- 1774: Cook takes a Tahitian, *Pa'i* back to Europe.
- 1773: Cook's second voyage to Tahiti.
- 1777: Cook's last voyage to Polynesia.
- 1788-1791: Mutiny on the 'Bounty.'
- 1793: beginning of the Pomare dynasty.

- 1797: arrival of the first missionaries from the 'London Missionary Society'.
- 1797: creation of the Pomare dynasty.
- 1815: the Polynesian chiefs lose the battle of *Fei Pi*. Pomare II is converted to Christianity.
- 1819: Pomare II creates the Pomare Code.
- 1836: English Protestants succeed in expelling the French missionaries.
- 1841: Depetit Thouar proclaims the French Protectorate of Tahiti.
- 1844-1847: Franco-Tahitian war.
- 1847: Pomare IV accepts the Protectorate of France.
- 1914-1918/1939-1945: numerous islanders set out to assist the French troops.
- 1958: the EFO (Establissments Français d'Océanie- French Establishments in Oceania) became French Polynesia.

Culture

Tahitians today have inherited a rich, expressive culture from their *ma'ohi* ancestors. From the *ma'ohi*, came the pulse of Tahitian life, a world where the lives of gods, warriors and men crossed in colorful legends. It's a place where the music and dance and art rose from the wonder of everyday island life. It's also where javelin throwing began as the sport of the gods, kings favored surf riding and men competed in canoe races and stone lifting as a show of pure strength.

Mana

Strength, power, influence, supremacy, greatness, sovereignty, omnipotence, prestige, control, genius, authority, superiority, nobility, stature, presence, elegance, beauty ... the list goes on an on.

These words define the Mana in a precise situation, a particular context, from a specific point of view. Mana is a mythical and essential concept, a fundamental truth. It's both tangible and intangible, expressive yet imperceptible, revealing but enigmatic, so natural but also mysterious and esoteric.

Mana lives, animates, raises up, ennobles and transcends every thing, every being, every element in every dimension; it can also annihilate, ruin and destroy until the last vital vibration.

Mana is seducing, enchanting, glamorous, penetrating, fascinating. The Mana is frightening, dangerous, consuming, lethal.

It is the root of the duality of life and death.

It is the essence of the universal power, the heart of the Polynesian universe, the beings bringing it to life, the elements shaping it, the existential, cultural and spiritual values which created the Polynesian/Ma'ohi who glorifies this universe.

The Mana is purity (*ma*); it arises from the life, humility, respect, dignity, love, sharing, beauty, goodness and peace of the beings and things that merge harmoniously in this *ma'ohi* universe.

The Mana is wisdom (*na/na'a*); it emanates from the empirical, technical and ancestral knowledge, from the common sense arising out of the inalienable link between man and his environment, from the faith in the divine, the state of grace that every thing and every being can reach through a spiritual, cultural and profane quest for the universal Mana, the promise to be reborn wiser, purer and more powerful.

Be pure, be wise and the Mana will live in you!

Tattoos

The word *tatau* originated in *The Islands of Tahiti*, and the symbols have meaning and the meaning tells the story of each Tahitian's personal history. In each line drawn on the body, the *ma'ohi* of the past is connected to the Mana of the present and future. The presence of Tohu, the god of *tatau*, who painted all the oceans' fish in their colors and patterns, gives each *tatau* an essence of meaning and life. A link between heaven and earth. In Polynesia, tattoos are also signs of beauty, and in earlier times were an important part of life as they signaled the end of adolescence.

Mythical Origins
There are a multitude of legends concerning the origins of the *tatau*. They all have one point in common: they are always a gift from a god to man. On the island of Tahiti, one of these legends tells how the first *tatau* were done on the sons of the god *Ta'aroa*, the supreme creator god of everything in the Polynesian firmament. The sons taught it to other men who made extensive use of it. As a result, the two sons of

Ta'aroa, *Matamata* and *Tū Ra'i Pō* became the patron divinities of tattooing.

Historical Origins

The origins of tattooing are quite vague, no doubt going back to the beginning of the *māori* civilization. Tattooing was probably already in existence among the successive waves of peoples who migrated from South East Asia, first to the eastern Polynesian islands, then the western islands, beginning in the second century BC. The practice seems to have existed in all the islands known jointly as the "Polynesian triangle," an area bounded by today's French Polynesia, New Zealand, Hawaii, Samoa, Easter Island and the Cook Islands. Tattooing was widely practiced and found in particular forms throughout French Polynesia, with the exception of the south of the Austral Islands and the east of the Tuamotu Islands. It was in the Marquesas Islands that the art of tattooing reached its peak of development in terms of its great richness and the complexity of its motifs.

Role In Traditional Society

In pre-European Polynesian society, tattooing constituted a valuable social marker. It could indicate one's exact place in a territory, tribe and family and one's level on the social scale. It could also mark the accomplishment of important social rituals such as the passage from childhood to puberty or marriage. It also could represent remarkable events in the life of the person concerned: acts of bravery in war or prowess as a hunter or fisherman. And it could be simply decorative. Its use was very widespread.

"Tattooing is not compulsory, but it would not have been considered acceptable for a Tahitian to have no tattoos at all," explained anthropologist Anne Lavondes, writing about tattooing in the Society Islands.

Different Types of Tattoos
One can distinguish three types of tattoo: those intended for gods, priests and *ari'i*, which are hereditary and therefore reserved for their descendants; those of the *hui ari'I* type, reserved for chiefs (men and women); those of the *hui to'a, hui ra'atira* and *'iato'ai, manahune* types, for war leaders, warriors, dancers, rowers and the like.

Sacred
One of the fundamental aspects of tattooing was its sacred nature. Believed to be inherited from the gods, tattooing carried with it supernatural power. Certain motifs were thought to protect man from the loss of his *mana*. They also represented the prestige and divine essence responsible for man's health, or of his equilibrium and fertility and from harmful influences.

Role in The Afterlife

Tattooing also went far beyond the life of this world. Being eternal, "this inalterable work inscribed on their skin would later bear witness to their origins, rank and heroism when they were called to appear before their ancestors: the gods of the mythical country of *Hawaiki*," explained Karl Von Den Steinen, a German ethnologist who undertook a detailed analysis in 1897-8 of the various forms of artistic expression of the peoples of the Marquesas Islands, including tattooing.

Specific to Each Archipelago

The different populations each developed their own specific designs and particular motifs. In the language of the Marquesas, tattooing is called *patu* tiki, which means "stamping with images." On this archipelago, the body could be entirely covered with tattoos, including the face. On the other hand, in the Leeward Islands, the face was never tattooed. Unfortunately, much of the meaning of the motifs and designs has been lost over time.

The Tools of Traditional Tattooing

The tools of traditional tattooing comprised a small serrated comb, made of bone, tortoiseshell or mother-of-pearl, fixed to a wooden handle. The teeth were soaked in ink based on charcoal from the *ti'a'iri*, or candlenut (*Aleurites Moluccana*), diluted in oil or water. The teeth were placed on the skin while the tattooist struck the handle with another piece of wood, causing the skin to break and the ink to penetrate. With these traditional tools, producing a tattoo could be extremely painful and took days, weeks, months or even years. This reinforced the role of the tattoo as a rite of passage.

Tattoo "Priests"

Being responsible for this delicate operation, the priest tattooist known as *tahu'a tatau*, in the Society Islands and *tuhuka patu* tiki in the Marquesas Islands, was paid handsomely and enjoyed great respect in traditional society. This status was often passed down from father to son.

Prohibition

As soon as they settled permanently in the Polynesian Islands at the end of the eighteenth century, both Catholic and Protestant missionaries fought against the practice of tattooing. *Pōmare* II, the second "king" of the dynasty of the same name, converted to Catholicism in 1812 and in 1819 drew up a code of rules which including the banning of tattoos. It is described as a practice which must be "completely abolished" as it "belonged to ancient and bad customs." As Polynesians now had to be fully clothed in the newly Christianized society, the very raison d'être of tattooing was largely disappearing. Consequently, the great majority of motifs as well as the technique itself of tattooing were lost forever.

Renewal

At the beginning of the '80s, the *tatau* once more occupied a major role in Polynesian society as this secular practice was re-appropriated and renewed. Of course, its sacred nature and role as a social marker, fundamental to traditional society, were considerably dimmed. Tattooing became the bearer of a determined reclaiming of the Polynesian identity, to which was obviously added an aesthetic dimension. Now, many young Polynesians get themselves tattooed.

Having explored and researched to try to rediscover the original meaning of the motifs a meaning which has been completely lost for many of them the Polynesian tattooists are now developing their art in three main directions: the reproduction of traditional motifs, the creation of strictly decorative motifs (such as dolphins or manta rays) and some have created motifs which are completely new, yet directly inspired from tradition.

International Recognition

Tattooists are now at work in nearly all the main inhabited islands of French Polynesia. Their reputation and the beauty of the Polynesian *tatau* are such that they attract visitors from elsewhere. Some Polynesian tattooists practice their art in many major cities of the world such as Paris, London or New York. Polynesian tattooing has gained an international reputation both because of its traditional roots and its very fashionable ethnic aesthetic.

Music and Dance

When the missionaries came to Tahiti, they tried to suppress the powerful, life-affirming and sensual sounds and movements that embody the music and dance of Tahiti. In the dance and rhythms, Tahitians give voice to their Mana, allowing it to rise from the sea, descend from the hills, and emanate from the soul of every man and woman who falls under its mesmerizing spell. Today's Tahitian dance and music celebrates the resilience of Polynesian culture to overcome and maintain their sacred expressions of life. In ancient times, dances were linked with all aspects of life. One would dance to welcome a visitor, to pray, to challenge an enemy or to seduce a mate.

Today's dance remains a powerful, potent symbol, especially when accompanied by the harmonic voices of the Tahitians, the thunder of traditional drums and plaintive song of conch shells.

Song

Traditional Instruments
Today's orchestras use percussion and stringed instruments. Among the percussion is the *to'ere*; the *fa'alete*; the *pahu* with two skins and

beaten with a stick and the *pahu tupa'i rima*, with one skin, that is played with the hands. The stringed instruments consist of the ukulele and the guitar.

Other instruments that had long disappeared have progressively made a come-back, those such as the *ihara*, a split bamboo drum and the *vivo*, a nasal flute. Finally, all sorts of sounds are obtained by clacking stones, from shells, by using *penu* (piion) or coconuts.

Other chants were secular and accompanied the events of everyday life. There are sound reminiscences of collective activities such as beating *tapa* (bark cloth). In the Marquesas Islands, the chants in religious ceremonies were often only understood by the priests, and were accompanied by drums and handclaps.

During festivals the chants progressively accompanied the beat initiated by the *pahu* drums. The rupture with the cultural past is most profound in the domain of music. Perhaps this is because no one bothered to write it down or perhaps it's because the European influence was imposed very early on without violence.

The European influence started with sailors and their profane songs and music. It continued with the missionaries who brought their canticles and hymns. The *himene* is a cross between the religious hymns imported by the first Protestant missionaries and polyphonic Tahitian chants that were sung before the arrival of Europeans.

The main forms of *himene* are *himene tarava*, *himene ru'au* and *ute*. The first two are rooted in English Protestant liturgy and in the pre-European period. Both types of musical expression generally praise a legendary god, a famous chief or protective animals. These songs use very poetic lyrics. Each island and district has its specific interpretations.

Dance

In pre-European Polynesia, dances "were many and varied" (W. Ellis, 1831), but little else is known about them. All we know is that both men and women danced, together or separately. Certain dances were performed standing up, others sitting down. Musicians used to accompany the dances with a limited number of instruments, essentially the *pahu* (drum with two skins) the *vivo*, a nasal flute.

Associated, as was tattooing, with nudity and therefore with immodesty, dancing was forbidden by missionaries. It was not until the 1950s that this ancestral art found its place again among Polynesian customs, and was reborn thanks to oral transmission and the writing of travelers.

Types of Dancing

In Tahitian dancing today there are, four types of dance.

- **The *Otea*:** this must have been originally a somewhat military dance, reserved for men. It has become the most famous of the Tahitian dances. It is choreographed around a theme and its musical accompaniment is performed on percussion and made up of rhythmical motifs called *pehe*.

- **The *Aparima*:** in this dance, the hands of the dancers mime history. The *aparima* can be either *vava*(silent) and consist of pantomime, generally performed while kneeling and accompanied by percussion or it can be sung, *aparima himene*, and the movements are in time to the chant which is accompanied by stringed instruments.

- **The *Hivinau*:** during this choreography, male and female dancers wend round in a circle and a male soloist voices a phrase that the choir takes up. The orchestra is made up of various drums and the pace is maintained by the dancers' songs.

- **The *Pa'o'a*:** this dance seems to be derived from the movements used to make *tapa* (a sort of parchment made from vegetable matter). Male and female dancers crouch down in a semi-circle. A male soloist voices a theme that the choir answers. A couple get up and perform a short dance in the circle to the sound of '*hi*'s and '*ha*'s.

The other archipelagos were greatly influenced by Tahitian dancing, but they have preserved certain of their own dances such as the bird dance in the Marquesas, *kapa* in the Tuamotus and *pe'i* in the Gambiers.

Crafts

The art of plaiting is found in various forms such as hats, bags baskets, mats etc. The women from the Austral Islands are noted as experts of this discipline that uses vegetal fibers from the screw pine, the coconut or the reed or *a'eho*.

The taste for observing and loving nature is revived in the sumptuous *tifaifai* or bed covers with hand-sewn vegetal or ethnic motifs. The enthusiasm of the women for this typical element of the decoration of fares or Polynesian homes is evidence of real creativity and has given rise to the organization of an annual show of *tifaifai*. Artistic expression also finds an outlet in woodwork, the prerogative of the men.

They sculpt, according to their inspiration, and according to ancestral, diagrammatic or symbolic patterns in precious wood: *tou* or local palisander, *miro* or rosewood. The Marquesans excel in this domain and produce superb pieces of work, spears, puzzles and *umete* which are fruit bowls in which special meals can be served.

Certain craftsmen sometimes resort to volcanic rock, corals and even bones to fashion a thousand decorations and useful items such as *penu* or pestles. Finally the revival of mother of pearl really shows the iridescent effects of the polished insides of shells. Their ever-changing, fascinating shades have made them choice decorative items to beautify dance costumes or make sparkling jewels.

Festivals & Events

Polynesian Art Jewelry For Christmas: From Tuesday December 20 To Saturday December 24 2017tahiti
The Polynesian handicraft art association puts on display some great skills and diverse handicraft work in the hall of the Assembly of French Polynesia. Association Bijouterie d'Art Polynésien Tel.: (689) 40.58.42.38 Faaura BOUTEAU GSM: (689) 87.75.03.63 fauuracreations@yahoo.fr

Christmas In The City: Mid-December 2017tahiti
The city of Papeete shimmers with lights on Boulevard Pomare on the waterfront and at the city hall as they nights comes in. Shops

contribute to the magic as they decorate their store fronts for Christmas, much to the excitement of kids and adults. Papeete Centre Ville CCISM Mairie de Papeete Tel. : (689).

Apetahi Raid: December 3 2017raiatea

This fantastic race in the middle of Raiatea's nature honors the 'Apetahi flower, which is becoming harder and harder to find. Indeed, the organizers, who are close to nature, wanted the competing runners and the media to realize how important it is to protect the flower. Association Fenua Loisirs Philippe DUBERNE GSM: (689) 87.75.47.36 .

Festival Makeva Anaa: Beginning Of December 2017other Tuamotu Islands

'Anaa atoll goes into action as they share their culture, their traditions and their skills with delegations from other islands ; The invited delegations perform dances and chants and prepare the Umu Ti fire walk and visit cultural sites. Comité organisateur Makeva Anaa Tel.: (689) 40.81.90.64 joana@mail.pf.

Tiare Day: Friday December 2 2017all Islands

The country's emblematic flower, the Tiare Tahiti, is celebrated with a flower decoration contest in which companies and public institutions take part with the theme "Garlands and bouquets of Tiare Tahiti".

Groupement de Solidarité des Femmes de Tahiti Tel.: (689) 40.43.20.66 GSM: (689) 87.74.42.00 Tahiti Tourisme Tel.: (689) 40.50.40.30 gsft@mail.pf, info@tahiti-tourisme.pf www.gsft.pf

The Rising Of The Pleiads: From November 20 2017all Islands

Matari'i i ni'a, when the season of abundance begins (tau 'auhune). The transition from one season to the other was a major moment in ancient society, where people would practice important rites and rituals. Association Haururu Vetea AVAEMAI Tel.: (689) 40.42.87.27 GSM: (689) 87.79.83.83 haururu.farefenua@mail.pf.

Hura Tapairu: Week From November 21 2017tahiti

Te Fare Tauhiti Nui celebrates the anniversary of this relatively recent competition which is drawing scores of traditional dance groups from everywhere. From the most famous dance groups to groups formed specifically for the occasion. Maison de la Culture Te Fare Tauhiti Nui Tel.: (689) 40.54.45.44 communication@maisondelaculture.pf www.maisondelaculture.pf.

Book Fair (14th Edition): Mid-November 2017tahiti

This fair aims at regrouping everyone who distributes and promotes reading books in French Polynesia during conferences, meetings with local and non-local authors, various entertainments, book sales exhibitions, etc. in the gardens and rooms of Te Fare Tauhiti Nui. Maison de la Culture Te Fare Tauhiti Nui Tel.: (689) 40 54 45 44.

Hawaiki Nui Va'a (24th Edition): From The 1st November To The 3rd Includedall Islands

In the leeward islands, the chief sport is the traditional paddling sport called Va'a outrigger canoe. Over 100 canoes paddle to Huahine, Raiatea, Taha'a and Bora Bora. The finish line is on the legendary beach of Matira Point (Bora Bora). Fédération Tahitienne de Va'a Tel.: (689) 40.45.05.44 ftvtutu@mail.pf www.hawaikinuivaa.pf.

Vaiparaoa Sapinus Surfing And Body-Boarding: From Wednesday October 12 To Sunday October 30 2017all Islands

Over a 3-week waiting period, with 4 to 5 days of competition 15 minutes from the airport, the city of Punaauia shows their 2nd surf spot: The coral barrier at Sapinus, where surf and body-board sessions go live. Taapuna Surf Club GSM: (689) 87.78.60.87 taapunamastertahiti@mail.pf taapunamaster.blogspot.com.

Reva I Eimeo Nui (2nd Edition): Saturday October 1 Or The First Saturday Of October 2017moorea

A must-do circle island tour of Moorea starting at the Papeete ferry docks to Vaiare wharf, riding "Le truck" to experience the sounds of the 'ukulele, stopping at various sites, all the way to your Tahitian meal awaiting The Ma'a Tahiti. Tahiti Tourisme Tel.: (689) 40.50.40.30 info@tahiti-tourisme.pf www.tahiti-tourisme.pf.

World Tourism Day: Tuesday September 27 2017all Islands

A Worldwide celebration that the 5 archipelagos celebrate too on a given theme from the WTO World Tourism Organization. Tourism professionals, the population and visitors celebrate this day on tourist sites entertained with dances, traditional music... Tahiti Tourisme Tel.: (689) 40.50.40.30 info@tahiti-tourisme.pf www.tahiti-tourisme.pf.

Farereihaga: From Monday September 19 To Saturday September 24 2017rangiroa

In Rangiroa in the Tuamotu islands, the big family of the hospitality sector celebrates everything connected to culture, fishing, handicraft along with multiple contests with the locals. Visitors are welcome and invited to experience the Farereihaga. Comité de tourisme de Rangiroa Tel.: (689) 40.93.11.30 philcabral@usa.net.

Agricultural Fair: Mid-September 2017all Islands

For fifteen days, the primary sector is put forward to the population, adults and young kids alike, with schools coming to discover farm animals and Polynesian local produce. A good number of exhibitors coming from the 5 archipelagos. Service du développement rural Tel.: (689) 40.42.81.44.

Super Aito Va'a (26th Edition): Saturday August 20 2017tahiti

Solo canoe race with the 100 best paddlers from "Te 'Aito" in two legs, Mahina Papeete and Taapuna pass. Association Ruahatu GSM: (689) 87.73.16.19 charley@mail.pf.

Painapo Raid (15th Edition): Saturday September 19 2017moorea

This is a two-person mountain run organized on Moorea island with 3 races scheduled: Toa race (18 km) Arearea race (7 km) and Family stroll (4 km). The courses change every year. Te Moorea Club Tel.: (689) 40.56.25.79 GSM: (689) 87.78.50.83.

Tahiti Nui Tour: From Wednesday August 24 To Sunday August 28 2017tahiti

Tahiti hosts this cycling tour, and adds Moorea island, which is a 30-minute boat ride away. Pacific delegations are expected to take part: Chili, New Zealand, Australia, New Caledonia... Fédération Tahitienne de Cyclisme GSM: (689) 87.79.83.09.

Trials Air Tahiti Nui Surfing / Billabong Pro Tahiti: From Friday August 12 To Tuesday August 24 2017tahiti

Qualifying surf competition at Teahupo'o on Tahiti's peninsula, prior to the famous Billabong Pro that brings together foreign and local surf professionals. Fédération Tahitienne de Surf Tel.: (689) 40.43.86.93 GSM: (689) 87.29.68.76 fedesurf@live.fr www.surf.pf.

Shows At Marae Arahurahu: Saturday August 6 2017tahiti

Shows on cultural history with "Te Aroha Mamaia" staged by professional dance group Toakura with the support of the Arts Conservatory of French Polynesia. Conservatoire Artistique de Polynésie française Te Fare Upa Rau Tel.: (689) 40.50.14.18 Fax: (689) 40.43.71.29 GSM: (689) 87.70.75.63 frederic@conservatoire.pf.

Areareara'a I Te Fenua Aihere (2nd Edition): Saturday July 30 2017tahiti

Half-circle island tour of Tahiti to the peninsula on two modes of transportation: A road trip aboard the traditional "Le Truck" then a boat ride with stops at public sites to the sounds of the 'ukulele. Tahiti Tourisme Tel.: (689) 40.50.40.30 info@tahiti-tourisme.pf www.tahiti-tourisme.pf.

Te Aito Va'a (29th Edition): From Friday July 22 To Saturday July 23 2017tahiti

A day of solo canoe races covering a distance of about 6 miles. The 100 best paddlers. Association Ruahatu GSM: (689) 87.73.16.19 charley@mail.pf.

Shows At Marae Arahurahu: Saturday July 9, 16, 23, 30 2017tahiti

Shows on cultural history with "Te Aroha Mamaia" staged by professional dance group Toakura with the support of the Arts

Conservatory of French Polynesia. Conservatoire Artistique de Polynésie française Te Fare Upa Rau Tel.: (689) 40.50.14.18 Fax: (689) 40.43.71.29 GSM: (689) 87.70.75.63 frederic@conservatoire.pf.

Heiva Mapuru A Paraita I Papeete: Mid-July 2017tahiti
Traditional dance groups who run for the Heiva i Tahiti perform around the Papeete Market. Direction du Marché de Papeete Tel.: (689) 40.43.67.15 Fax: (689) 40.43.67.98
jeannot.loshing@villedepapeete.pf, pcv@mail.pf.

Bastille Day: July 14 2017all Islands
Bastille Day celebration is organized in the same way as in all French territories, with a military march to which all the authorities are invited. The Islands of Tahiti also celebrate this Republican event. Communication du Haut-Commissariat Tel.: (689) 40.46.87.51 www.polynesie-francaise.pref.gouv.fr.

Heiva I Tahiti (136th Edition): From July 7 To July 23 2017all Islands
The best chant and dance groups compete on the famous Toata stage and rival with creativity to showcase the most festive and rooted Polynesian traditions. This competition dates back to 1881 and fosters a spirit of unity between the artists and the spectators. Maison de la Culture Te Fare Tauhiti Nui Tel.: (689).

Fire Walk On Umu Ti: Wednesday July 6 2017tahiti

Every year, a big underground oven is dug to cook the Ti plant in the traditional fashion thanks to heated stones on which people experience the fire walk under the blessing of the Great Priest of the ceremony. Raymond GRAFFE GSM: (689) 87.78.54.75 www.heiva.pf

Us Independence Day Celebrations: From Saturday July 2 To July 4 2017tahiti

The commune of Mahina celebrates Independence Day at Venus Point with associations who boast the Made in USA: Harley Davidson riders, big cubes, football, base ball… Ville de Mahina Xavier ETAETA Tel. : (689) 40.48.11.35 xavieretaeta@yahoo.fr.

Sport Competition Of The Heiva: From Friday July 1 2017tahiti

Multi-category V1 (solo), V3, V6 and V16 sprint races at Tehoro beach in Mataiea, followed by a marathon course between Tahiti and Moorea. On other days, don't miss the famous traditional sailing canoe races and traditional sports Tu'aro Ma'ohi in Tahiti. Maison de la Culture Te Fare Tauhiti Nui Tel.: (689) 40.54.45.44.

International Golf Open: Beginning Of July 2017tahiti

Located some 30 miles away from Papeete (Tahiti), the Olivier Bréaud golf course extends in the vast 'Atimaono domain of Papara and hosts, every year, one of the stops of the Pacific tour organized by the

Australian PGA. Fédération Polynésienne de Golf Tel.: (689) 87.77.17.41 louis.lesourd@gmail.com.

Heiva In The Outer Islands: July 2017tahiti

Some islands like Moorea, Huahine, Maupiti, Rurutu proudly celebrate their cultures with inter-district activities to highlight their talent in chants, dance, sports... Comités de tourisme et Mairies info@tahiti-tourisme.pf.

Internal Self-Government Day: Wednesday June 29 2017tahiti

Sports and cultural associations parade and march Hivavaevae in Papeete city ; 32nd anniversary. Maison de la Culture Te Fare Tauhiti Nui Tel. : (689) 40.54.45.44 communication@maisondelaculture.pf www.heiva.pf.

The Orange Festival In Punaauia: Saturday June 25 2017tahiti

Punaauia city celebrates the orange fruits from the Tamanu plateau. Service des sports et de la jeunesse de la Ville de Punaauia Tel.: (689) 40.86.56.56 www.punaauia.pf.

Heiva Rimai (Handicrafts): From Friday June 24 2017tahiti

Traditional handicraft experts from the 5 island groups of French Polynesia stay all in one place for a month-long exhibition of their handicraft products. Most of the materials used come from their islands and they are truly "Made in Tahiti". Service de l'artisanat Tel.: (689) 40.54.54.00 secretariat@artisanat.gov.pf www.artisanat.pf.

World Music Day: Week Of June 21 2017tahiti

For over a decade now, artists, music lovers and music groups share their passion as they get together on private and public places around the world. Maison de la Culture Te Fare Tauhiti Nui Tel.: (689) 40.54.45.44 communication@maisondelaculture.pf info@tahiti-tourisme.pf.

Tahiti Moorea Sailing Rendez-Vous: From Friday June 24 To Sunday June 26 2017tahiti

The TMS has been designed to welcome tourists, amateur yachtsmen and the locals as they join in this 3-day event: One day on Tahiti for the welcoming celebration, one day for the sailing rally and one day on Moorea to experience traditional sport competition. Archipelagoes GSM: (689) 87.28.08.44 archipelagoes@mail.pf.

4th Annual Australia-Tahiti Event: Friday June 24 2017tahiti

Following the morning meeting between luxury yachting professionals near Marina Taina in Punaauia, the crews chill out with fun games and sports and fine food offered to get a sample of the tastes of the region. Tahiti Crew GSM: (689) 87.21.59.80 Fax: (689) 40.42.86.06 tahiticrew@mail.com fb : Tahiti-Crew.

Heiva I Bora Bora: From July 17 To July 24 2017bora Bora

The Heiva i Bora Bora is an annual dance, chant and traditional sports competition with handicraft exhibition and takes place at Tahua Moto'i in Vaitape. Comité de tourisme de Bora Bora Tel.: (689) 40.67.76.36 GSM: (689) 87.73.54.22 info-bora-bora@mail.pf.

Miss Tahiti Pageant: Friday June 24 2017tahiti

On that evening, the beauty queen of The Islands of Tahiti is elected among a slew of contenders and wins her ticket to the Miss France pageant at the end of year. Miss Tahiti shall remain available to the public for the various events she shall support. Comité Miss Tahiti Tel.: (689) 40.45.45.45 –.

Tahiti Fashion Week: From Wednesday June 8 To Friday June 10 2017tahiti

This fashion event is packed with innovation crafted by local and creative handicraft talents rivaling with one another with shows and model contests where people from the fashion world meet. Laurence JOUTAIN GSM: (689) 87.28.65.98 Alberto VIVIAN GSM: (689) 87.78.85.90.

Tahiti Moorea Marathon: Saturday June 4 2017moorea

This international marathon is run on Moorea island with 3 races scheduled: Marathon, Half-Marathon and Fenua Run (4km). The courses change every year. Te Moorea Club Tel.: (689) 40.56.25.79 GSM: (689) 87.78.50.83 contact@mooreamarathon.com.

The Vanilla Week: Mid-June 2017tahiti

Tahitian Vanilla will be celebrated over a few days as many vanilla growers from across the country meet together. Workshops on the many facets of Vanilla are organized and experts travel from the outer islands to express their pride for that black gold. Etablissement de la Vanille Tel.: (689) 40.50.89.50 Fax: (689) 40.50.89.52 vanille@vanilledetahiti.pf.

The Floralies: End Of May 2017tahiti

Meeting place for flower fans, shrub lovers and seekers of endemic tree offshoots. It's the perfect moment to detect the rarest or the most sought after plant varieties as the exhibition at Motu Ovini lasts 3 weeks. Service du développement rural Tel.: (689) 40.42.81.44

Tuaro Maohi: May And June 2017tahiti

Championship Qualifiers by traditional sports category for men and women in the run-up to the Heiva. Fédération des sports et jeux traditionnels Amuitahira'a Tu'aro Maohi Tel.: (689) 87.77.09.05 enoch@mail.pf fb : Tu'aro Maohi.

Mother's Day: End Of May 2017all Islands

Shops, restaurants and tourism accommodation providers offer specials and discounts on various products to spoil every mum in on their special day. Papeete Centre Ville CCISM Mairie de Papeete Tel.: (689) 40.47.27.38 Fax: (689) 40.47.27.27 Marie@ccism.pf, pcv@mail.pf

Pareu Day: Friday May 27 2017all Islands
Pareu Day is celebrated everywhere around the world since the day a small group of Polynesians launched it in 2013 with the help of social networks. The slot time for this monthly festive event taking place in Papeete city is on the last week of May. Tahiti Tourisme Tel.: (689) 40.50.40.30 info@tahiti-tourisme.pf www.tahiti-tourisme.pf.

Mother's Day Show: From Monday 23 To Sunday May 29 2017tahiti
Let's meet at the Papeete city hall to find the perfect gift for mum. Association Bijouterie d'Art Polynésien Faaura BOUTEAU GSM: (689) 87.75.03.63 fauuracreations@yahoo.fr.

La Ronde Tahitienne 5th Edition: Sunday May 22 2017tahiti
From the Fautaua velodrome in Pirae to the circle island tour of Tahiti, the Vélo Club de Tahiti and VSOP associations now organize the 5th edition of La Ronde Tahitienne. Vélo club de Tahiti GSM: (689) 87.73.36.17 benito@mail.pf www.larondetahitienne.pf.

The Rising Of The Pleiads: From Friday May 20 2017all Islands
"Matari'i i raro", where the food shortage season starts. The transition

from one season to the other was a major moment in ancient society, where people would practice important rites and rituals. Association Haururu Vetea AVAEMAI Tel.: (689) 40.42.87.27 GSM: (689) 87.79.83.83 haururu.farefenua@mail.pf.

X Terratahiti (8th Edition): Saturday May 14 2017tahiti
Vélo club de Tahiti and VSOP are two associations who organize a competition centered around the environment and fair-play. The competition is on two days and the circuit follows several iconic sites of Tahiti. Association sportive VSOP GSM: (689) 87.77.24.99 vsop@mail.pf www.xterratahiti.com.

Ono'u International Graffiti Art Festival: From Monday May 2 To Sunday May 8 2017tahiti
It is the most important international event in the Pacific region for urban contemporary art and takes place in May. ONO'U regroups about fifty renowned graffiti artists coming from every corner of the world. Société Tahiti Nouvelles Générations GSM: (689) 87.70.41.42 sarah.roopinia@gmail.com www.tahitifestivalgraffiti.com.

Taapuna Master Surfing (22nd Edition): From Saturday May 7 To Sunday May 29 2017tahiti
A big Open reef surf competition for non-professional surfers spread over 6 days at Taapuna pass in Punaauia two days reserved to Juniors

on May 7-8, to wait for the best waves. Taapuna Surf Club GSM: (689) 87.78.60.87 taapunamastertahiti@mail.pf taapunamaster.blogspot.com.

Hiva Oa Marathon: Friday May 6 2017marquesas Islands
A run from Puamau village to Atuona village. Comité du tourisme de Hiva oa Tel.: (689) 40.92.78.93 GSM: (689) 87.24.79.75 Comitetourismehivaoa@marquises.pf.

Tahiti Pearl Regatta (13th Edition): From Monday 2 To Sunday May 8 2017raiatea
This is a colorful regatta between Raiatea, Taha'a and Bora Bora islands, that is open to all kinds of sailboats, with people from many countries, and which combines races in the open sea and inside the lagoons. Archipelagoes GSM: (689) 87.79.54.44 tpr@mail.pf

'Ukulele Festival: Mid-April 2017tahiti
The World record was crushed last year by Tahiti as 4 750 players gathered on April 11 2015. This event is an occasion to show the different shapes and sonorities of 'ukulele instruments. Maison de la Culture Te Fare Tauhiti Nui Tel.: (689) 40.54.45.44 communication@maisondelaculture.pf www.maisondelaculture.pf.

Festival Pro Surf At Papara: Week From April 11 2017tahiti
Surf competition with international youth from the WQS professional

circuit World Qualify Series on the beach at Taharuu Papara in the Junior, Open and Ondines categories. Fédération Tahitienne de Surf Tel.: (689) 40.43.86.93 GSM: (689) 87.29.68.76 fedesurf@live.fr

Raid Vanira (7th Edition): Saturday April 9 2017tahaa
15 km run across the lush nature of Taha'a island (Leeward Islands) in the Associated Commune of Hipu. Music performances, fruit tasting, handicraft stalls, food stands.. AS Tahaa Vanira Jack BENNETT GSM: (689) 87.78.23.41 bennett.jack@mail.pf.

Pro Rangiroa Junior Surf: Week From April 4 2017rangiroa
A professional surf competition for the Junior category in Rangiroa and organized under the umbrella of the Commune of Rangiroa in partnership with the tourism sector. Comité de Tourisme de Rangiroa Tel.: (689) 40.93.11.30 GSM: (689) 87.78.79.78 rangiroa-tourisme@mail.pf.

Earth Hour (4th Edition): Saturday March 19 2017all Islands
An event on environmental issues to encourage people to save on energy consumption by taking symbolic actions on the theme of going back to the roots, replacing light with ancient and fun ingredients on Tahiti island, with its peninsula, as well as Moorea. Représentant Earth Hour GSM: (689) 87.77.22.87 jerry.biret@gmail.com.

International Women's Day: Tuesday March 8 2017all Islands

A lot of initiatives done to value and defend the cause of Polynesian women. Tel.: (689) 40 80 00 40.

Arrival Of The Evangelists: Saturday March 5 2017all Islands

Commemoration of the arrival of the first British protestant missionaries in Matavai Tahiti. This year marks the 219th anniversary of the establishment of the Gospel. Eglise Protestante Maohi Tel.: (689) 40.46.06.00 choiore@epm.pf.

Tahiti Festival Guitare (9th Edition): From February 25 To February 27 2017tahiti

The "Tahiti Espoirs Guitare" is a contest for Tahiti's best young guitar player. Great nights in perspective as international artists join the finalists. Collectif Tahiti Rock GSM: (689) 87.73.50.55 leomarais@mail.pf www.tahitifestivalguitare.org.

Valentine's Day Show: From February 8 To February 13 2017all Islands

Discover the most creative and diverse Polynesian handicraft at the Polynesian Art Association Show with jewels, artefact's and clothing. Meeting point at the Assembly of French Polynesia. Association Bijouterie d'Art Polynésien Tel.: (689) 40.58.42.38 Faaura BOUTEAU GSM: (689) 87.75.03.63 fauuracreations@yahoo.fr.

Chinese New Year: February 8 2017all Islands

The Chinese community of French Polynesia celebrates the year of the "Fire Monkey". During the festivities, all the country's rich Chinese culture and folklore are highlighted through dances, cooking, arts and ancestral rites. Association Si Ni Tong Tel.: (689) 40.42.74.18 sinitong@mail.pf.

Flower And Handicraft Festival: From Monday February 1st To Sunday February 14 2017tahiti

Neighborhoods exhibit their flowers and jewels in a scentful and colorful atmosphere in the gardens of the Papeete City Hall, perfect for the lovers' celebration. Associations des quartiers de Papeete GSM: (689) 87.77.54.37 adams.myrna@yahoo.fr.

The Pacific International Documentary Film Festival Of Tahiti Fifo (13th Edition): From January 30 To February 7 2017tahiti

This time-honored festival gathers audiovisual documentary works about Oceania in front of an international jury and has film screening, free workshops, conferences and meetings scheduled over a few days. Maison de la Culture Te Fare Tauhiti Nui Tel.: (689) 40.54.45.44 organisation@filmfestivaloceanie.org www.fifotahiti.org.

Tere Fa'ati (11th Edition): January 30 2017 Tahiti

Circle island tour of Tahiti on the traditional "Le Truck" bus cruising to the sound of the 'ukulele with stops at tourist sites, such as those designed by Tahiti Tourisme. Tahiti Tourisme Tel.: (689) 40.50.40.30 info@tahiti-tourisme.pf www.tahiti-tourisme.pf.

Tere A'ati: From January 2 To January 8 2017tahiti
A cultural and historic event which takes place on Rurutu in the Austral islands where people go for a long walk with stops at ancestral sites archaeological sites and cliffs, etc. to the 3 villages Moerai, Avera and Auti and visit different homes. Comité du Tourisme de Rurutu

Religion

Religious Beliefs. Just as with Tahitian society, native Religion recognized a ranked series of gods starting with one supreme deity and passing down through lesser gods and subordinates to individual family spirits of departed relatives. Religion was centered on regional, tribal, and kin tutelar deities, although a few of the gods transcended such limitations and were, in effect, supratribal deities. Gods required a wide variety of appeasements in order to ensure the continued welfare of the individual as well as the tribe. Early nineteenth century missionary activity successfully substituted Christian beliefs for the earlier traditional ones.

Religious Practitioners. Aboriginally, priests were of the chiefly class and were of two kinds. There were those who conducted formal rituals during which the gods were prayed to and appeased by gifts in order to gain their favor. Others were inspirational priests through whom particular gods spoke and offered oracular advice. All priests received some sort of payment for their activities and many were believed to have powers of sorcery. With the nineteenth-century acceptance of Christianity, various Tahitians, not all necessarily of the chiefly class, were trained by the missionaries to become lay preachers.

Ceremonies. Religious ceremonies were carried out in marae, most of which were tabooed to women. Some Ceremonies were seasonal affairs, while others pertained to war and peace, thanksgiving, atonement, and critical life-cycle events of chiefs. The degree of ceremonialism was dependent upon the deity and the importance of the marae, those for Commoners in districts and smaller land divisions being the least elaborate

Ade Pearson

Travel and Tourism

With so many options, you can do as much or as little as you like. The Islands of Tahiti, officially known as French Polynesia, possesses one of the most spectacularly beautiful and diverse environments on earth. A mixture of high volcanic islands and low-lying atolls, these specks of land 118 islands in all are strewn across four million square km of the South Pacific. Clustered into five archipelagos: the Society Islands, the Tuamotu Islands, the Gambier Islands, the Marquesas Islands and the Austral Islands, The Islands of Tahitihave in common a delightful blend of Polynesian and French cultures, and a consistently tropical climate.

French Polynesia's world of oceanic islands offers vacationers an almost limitless range of vacation activities, both passive and active.

There are many sides to The Islands of Tahiti. Yet they are all connected by Mana. Mana is a life force and spirit that surrounds us. You can see it. Touch it. Taste it. Feel it. And from the moment you arrive, you will understand why we say our islands are Embraced by Mana.

Here, you'll find it all. From paragliding to beach combing to embracing the laid-back island lifestyle, The Islands of Tahiti are packed with a mix of tropical adventure and blissful relaxation. Stay in overwater bungalows to experience true island living while you're here. Or go snorkeling to get up close and personal with the local wildlife. If you're feeling even more daring, take a trip to swim with the sharks! Shop for cultured pearls, take a cruise, play a few rounds of golf, enjoy a motu picnic with the family there's so much to do in The Islands of Tahiti that you'll never want to leave.

Attraction and Activities
Diving & Snorkeling

Proudly displayed on the bodies of Tahitians, you'll find manta ray, shark, whale and sea turtle tattoos that tell the story of a people defined by the sea. Divers come from around the world to experience these sacred sea creatures, which, in *The Islands of Tahiti*, hold a place of reverence among the gods.

It's only natural that the sea around these islands is both figuratively and literally a clear blue heaven on earth. The warm waters that surround *The Islands of Tahiti* teem with life from flirty clown fish to ever-present sharks to awe-inspiring humpback whales, which arrive between July and November. When you're ready to do some diving and snorkeling, the heavens await.

The ocean represents the complete lifecycle to the Tahitians, and they have a masterful, reverential and respectful relationship with it. Traditional outrigger canoes, surfing and sailing are part of everyday life here in *The Islands of Tahiti*. Of course, travelers can also experience sunset cruising, kayaking, jet skiing and more. The sea, the rainforest and heaven are considered the realms of the gods in the Tahitian spiritual worlds, and we bet you'll agree once you visit us.

Island Dive Site Highlights

There are dozens of unique dive sites around each island and atoll and expert certified dive operators will take care of all the details. Dives and activities can be arranged in advance by your Preferred Travel Professional or through your resort or cruise ship.

Marine Environment

The crystal-clear waters of *The Islands of Tahiti* are home to more than 1,000 species of fish with an unmatched variety of color, size and shape. The smallest fish are often the most colorful and prefer the coral gardens and shallow depths of lagoons while larger species enjoy the bustle of life in the inlets and reef complexes and out in the open sea.

The combination of canyons, caverns and coral beds provides a multitude of nooks and crannies for marine life.

2,5 million sq. miles (4 million km²) natural aquarium

Because of its exceptional biodiversity, scientists consider the Polynesian sea zone to be the "richest aquarium on earth". In 2000, the entire region was classified as an Exclusive Economic Zone (EEZ), a wildlife sanctuary where, among other things, drift fishing is prohibited, earning French Polynesia top honors from the WWF (World Wildlife Fund).

The jade and turquoise waters of the lagoons of the Tuamotu and the Society Islands archipelagos, where slender, multi-colored fish species have evolved, attract nearly a third of all dolphin species from every ocean. Schools of damselfish, mullet and soldierfish frolic in the coral lacework as striped convict surgeonfish and frowning Picasso triggerfish pass by.

Manta rays, gliding across the shimmering sea bottom, can suddenly leap skyward and re-enter the water right next to placid sharks basking in the lagoons. Sea turtles bury their eggs in the warm sands of deserted beaches as whales mate and calve in the undisturbed bays of our archipelagos: the Austral Islands, the Gambier Islands, the Tuamotu and the Society Islands.

Marine Life
Whales (Tahitian Name: *Tohora*)
- The eternal migration

    Every year, from July to November, humpback whales (megaptera novaeangliae) migrate from the icy waters of the Antarctic where they feed to the warm waters of the shores of The Islands Of Tahiti. It is the ideal place to give birth and breed, sheltered from their predators. The adults measure between 40 to 60 feet (15 to 18 meters). They look very graceful while moving their huge pectoral fins under the water. The calves measure about 15 feet (4.50 meters) at birth. They can put on up to 220 lbs. (100 kg) per day during the first week of life, whale's milk contains the highest fat content of the animal kingdom. As a cetacean (whale) sanctuary since May 2002, all whales of French Polynesia are protected. Whale watching complies with strict local regulations.

- Where can I watch whales in The Islands of Tahiti?

    Although you can spot them from any island, Rurutu is a good location for whale watching. You should have an experienced guide who holds an official government authorization lead your whale watching expedition.

> How can I watch whales in The Islands of Tahiti?
> Bubbles are a sign of aggressiveness to marine mammals. Scuba diving is, therefore, not the best way to approach them. You are likely to experience a once in a lifetime encounter with only your snorkeling gear. For you and the whales' safety always follow your guide's instructions when you are in their presence.

Dolphins (Tahitian Name: *Ou'a*)

As a cetacean sanctuary, the dozen dolphin species of French Polynesia are also protected. They are present year round and can be seen around any of the islands. Dolphins behave very similarly to humans. They give birth, nurse their calves and breathe air. Their communication skills are very sophisticated. You're highly likely to encounter some of them during your stay in *The Islands of Tahiti*. Three main species are easily watched depending on the areas: bottle nosed dolphins (*tursiops truncatus*), spinner dolphins (*stenella longirostris*) and rough toothed dolphins (*steno bredanensis*).

Sharks (Tahitian Name: *Ma'o)*

Out of the 350 species known worldwide, 19 of them can be observed in the waters of French Polynesia, which is a perfect place for any diver to encounter them. It is also the ideal place to remove some of the myths surrounding sharks. The most commonly encountered species in *The Islands of Tahiti* are the famous black tip sharks (*carcharhinus melanopterus* Tahitian name: *ma'o mauri*), grey sharks (*carcharhinus amblyrhynchos* Tahitian name: *raira*), lemon sharks (*negaprion acutidens*, Tahitian name: *arava*) and hammerhead sharks (*sphyrna lewini* or *sphyrna mokarran* Tahitian name: *ma'o tuamata*).

➢ **The *ma'o* and the ancient Polynesians**

From antiquity to today, the western world has viewed sharks as bloodthirsty animals. Yet, the ancient ma'ohi lived with them in harmony. Sharks represented a protective icon in which the kind spirit of a family ancestor was reincarnated.

➢ **Essential to the oceans' eco-system**

Sharks belong at the top of the food chain and are generally either predators (population controllers) or scavengers and cleaners. They play an essential role in regulation and balance of the marine eco-systems. Thought to have evolved about 400 million years ago, these fish are extremely well developed and perfectly adapted to their environment. Having had no predator for millions of years, the rate of breeding is slow and quite inefficient. Depending on the species, a female's gestation can take four to 24 months with a potential fertilization only taking place every couple of years.

> **Are sharks endangered?**
Overfishing, pollution and killing sharks for their fins represent some of the many threats factors threatening and endangering sharks. According to scientific data, it's estimated that more than 150 million sharks are killed each year. Some species are already nearly extinct. To mitigate this problem, French Polynesia government made the decision to protect them by law in 2006.

Sea Turtles (Tahitian Name: Honu)

Two main turtle species live in French Polynesia and are easily encountered in some dive spots. The green turtle (chelonia mydas) owes its name to the color of its flesh and fat. The female reaches sexual maturity between 15 and 20 years of age. She can measure 60 inches (1.50 meters) and weigh up to 441 lbs. (200 kg). The juveniles are carnivorous, but become herbivorous once they are adults. The hawksbill turtle (eretmochelys imbricata) is smaller and does not measure more than 35 inches (90 cm) for a weight of 198 lbs. (90kg). Carnivorous, they are often found searching for small sponges stuck under rocks. They move using these rocks using their frontal legs. Oviparian, they have a slow reproduction cycle and a late sexual maturity. There are less and less laying sites due to loss of habitat from human development and they are the victims of drift net fishing and hunting. Turtles are now in danger of extinction worldwide. Numerous consciousness-raising campaigns are promoted in The Islands of Tahiti to ensure their conservation.

Rays (Tahitian Name: *Fai)*

Belonging to the elasmobranch family, rays are close cousins to the sharks. They appeared about 150 million years ago. Like the sharks, they have a cartilaginous skeleton. Yet, they are quite different: their branchial slits are located on the belly and their oversized pectoral fins are welded to their head enabling propulsion. This is what makes them look so gracious, appearing almost like underwater birds. Like their cousins, they have two sexual appendices called pterygopods. Three species of rays can be found easily in *The Islands of Tahiti:* sting rays (*himantura fai* Tahitian name: *fai i'u*), eagle rays (*aétobaus narinar* Tahitian name: *faimanu*) and manta rays (*manta birostris* Tahitian name : *fafapiti*). A couple of other manta species may also be seen: *himantura* sp. In the Marquesas and *mobula tarapacana*, a pelagic kind of manta ray bound to be encountered in the Tuamotu, Gambier and Marquesas.

Diving

Around all *The Islands of Tahiti*, dramatic views continue below the water. Divers and snorkelers are amazed by the density of large marine life. Regular encounters include manta rays whose gigantic wingspan eclipses the passing diver; schools of dolphin dancing along the surf; sharks seemingly at every turn; and, in the Austral Islands, humpback whales thrill the lucky spectators in their annual parade.

Underwater Photography

Whether you are a professional photographer or an amateur, French Polynesia is a perfect place for your passion. Indeed, the underwater clarity and visibility are excellent. A wide-angle lens is ideal for capturing your amazing encounters with the sharks and other pelagic fish. Those who enjoy macro photography will also be thrilled. *The Islands of Tahiti* are famous worldwide for the opportunities to capture amazing images of humpback whales either through video or photography. To protect yourself from paying duty taxes arriving and returning home you should carry copies of your camera's (and their accessories) purchase receipts in order to avoid any inconvenience with customs.

Fun Dives

Many dive centers work with an underwater cameraman. He will join your group during the dives and create a customized DVD to commemorate your dive in *The Islands of Tahiti*.

Professional Video & Shooting

The Islands of Tahiti have an abundance of specialized equipment and professionals to assist you in organizing shooting underwater images or TV documentaries. Some local producers have a wide range of experience in their field and an excellent set of references. Most bring with them a technically competent team, who will also be able to provide you with HD video cameras with underwater housing. Each island is a nature's underwater studio

The Other Aquatic Activities

Aquascopes

In Tahiti, Moorea and Bora Bora, glass-bottom boats and 'aquascopes' (a panoramic room situated under the bridge of the boat) make it possible to discover things hidden under the surface of the lagoon while staying dry. It's a totally original adventure that provides great opportunities to photograph aquatic landscapes. Small underwater vehicles are the ideal means of transport to go down 150 feet (50 meters) deep, and observe in detail the underwater depths without getting wet.

Helmet Diving

Diving with a helmet gives you the opportunity to take an aquatic excursion to a depth of 12 feet (3-4 meters). This activity does not require any level of diving skills or knowledge of classic diving equipment because your helmet is constantly connected to the surface. Accompanied by a qualified instructor, those who journey downwards explore the depths of the sea at their own pace, walking through the fields of coral.

Underwater Scooter

Fun and very accessible, the underwater scooter requires no diving experience. Just like their land-based versions, underwater scooters are propelled by electric motors, to a depth of 9 feet (3 meters), and can seat two passengers who can talk using a communal dome. This activity is available in Bora Bora.

Outdoors

There are so many ways to discover the outdoors in *The Islands of Tahiti*, and so many opportunities for hikes and excursions in island valleys or over hilltops where the breathtaking views encompass a full 360-degree panorama of mountains, bays, lagoons and on the horizon, the immense Pacific.

From canoeing to paddle boarding to soaring over the sea on a paraglider, you'll never find a shortage of things to do in the great outdoors in *The Islands of Tahiti*. Explore your options here.

How Can I explore The Islands of Tahiti?

Activities On Land:

On Foot:

In the high islands, you'll discover many walking tracks that lead to amazing lookout points, winding through wild valleys and undergrowth, in the shade of *mape* trees (Tahitian chestnut trees) as you search for the mysterious marae or religious places. Guides are qualified, offer high quality services and will keep you safe.

On Horseback:

Across spectacular landscapes with the valleys and the plateaux of the Marquesas islands, rich in archaeological remains, or along the white sand beaches (Tahiti, Huahine, Moorea and more), with the sun setting as a backdrop, or even going upstream from the rivers, crossing dense vegetation (Raiatea, Tahaa and more).

By Bike:

While a normal bike is ideal for the flat ring road, you'll want a mountain bike for making your way into the interior of the islands. Many hotels offer them for hire.

By 4×4 / Quad Bikes:

Excursions in off-road vehicles make it easy to effortlessly explore the mountainous, inner isles. Cars, scooters, "fun cars" and quad bikes are also available for hire in certain islands.

Adventures in The Air:

Skydiving

Free-fall for an unforgettable experience as you enjoy the view above the lagoons of Moorea, Bora Bora or Tahiti. Skydiving jumps take place in tandem with a professional skydiving instructor. You can find skydiving tour operators on Moorea, Bora Bora and Tahiti (at sunset).

Parasailing

Find yourself amazed by the turquoise waters. This is a novel way to enjoy the view from the sky, solo or in tandem, towed by a cable up to 900 feet long. Flying 600 feet above an improbable palette of turquoise is an experience you'll remember forever. This activity is offered by Mahana Parasail in Bora-Bora and Moorea.

A Helicopter Tour of the Islands

Exploring the islands from high in the sky is simply stunning: the view of the basalt peaks and the alignment of the ridges and plateaus reveals a unique facet of the islands' interior while the lagoons display a spectacular array of bright colors. Tours of Tahiti, Moorea and Bora

Bora are available (including a pass over Tupai, a heart-shaped atoll what's more romantic than that?). Tours to other destinations are also available upon request.

Aerobatics and Flying Lessons

If you're a thrill-seeker, then aerobatics are for you. After taking off from Tahiti-Faa'a airport with a pilot-instructor, you'll have the opportunity to improve your flying skills high above the lagoon. Lessons are offered at every level, from beginner to pilot's license. Just want to kick back and enjoy the view? Discovery flights around Tahiti are also available on request.

Paragliding

A completely safe tandem overflight of Tahiti, its steep-sided valleys, its plateaus and its lagoon. Paragliding is an affordable sport that is available to all ages with no particular physical fitness requirement.

Water Activities:

Surfing, Stand-up Paddle Boarding and Bodyboarding:

Whether it's surfing, stand up paddle or bodyboarding Polynesia is a paradise for surfers of all levels, both beginners and professionals. It provides a multitude of locations, ranging from the waves on the beach to the most dangerous waves over coral reefs and passes. The island of Tahiti alone has more than thirty surfing spots, of which three are world famous: Teahuppo, Taapuna and Maraa. In the southern winter (May to November), the best waves unfurl over the north coast while the south coast takes the waves for the rest of the year. Moorea, with the Tema'e site on its east coast, is also excellent. Finally, there are still secret spots in the islands frequented by pros and locals, mostly in the Tuamotu and Marquesas Islands.

Kitesurfing, Funboarding and Wind Surfing:
Whether it's kitesurfing, funboarding or wind surfing in Tahiti and in the islands, even the smallest breath of wind and a hint of sun are enough to bring out the kiteboards and windsurfers. These sports are very popular and it's easy to see why. They are 100 percent ecological and they open up new horizons for lovers of nautical adventures. *The Islands of Tahiti* combine all the ingredients that let you fully appreciate these disciplines, whatever your level. Go water sporting on calm, safe waters learn on the lagoons to start with, then increase speed and cover distance; and then on waves for surfing and jumping. And all this, together with a tropical climate, warm, crystal-clear water and breath-taking landscapes.

Outrigger Canoeing and Sailing:
Whether it's outrigger canoeing or sailing the lagoons with their calm waters offer tons of opportunities for sailing and anchoring. So,

everything from the traditional outrigger canoe to the racing course pirogue, from the great sailing ship to the simple kayak navigates over this marine paradise. These boats can be hired in most of the islands, including Taha'a and Raiatea.

Romance

The Islands of Tahiti are surely the prototype for the concept of the far-flung, south seas romantic escape: archipelagos of volcanic islands isolated in a gigantic blue ocean, protected entirely by barrier reefs that form some of the world's most fabled lagoons.

Hundreds of empty white-sand beaches fringe these still turquoise waters, while the forest-covered mountains of French Polynesia's dramatic volcanic hinterland rise hundreds sometimes thousands of feet into the blue skies above.

It's impossible not to get swept up in the romance of T*he Islands of Tahiti*. Whether it's new-found love or the rekindling of an old romance, you'll find the perfect backdrop for your next romantic adventure here.

French Polynesia is the ideal location for couples looking to relax on vacation. It also offers rare treats for couples who prefer to explore the adventurous side of *The Islands of Tahiti*.

French Polynesia's day spas are among the Pacific's best, offering traditional Polynesian massage techniques using local coconut and vanilla oils. The world's freshest seafood at some of the South Pacific's most prestigious restaurants is served right beside lagoons or delivered right to you (by outrigger canoe, if you wish) on the deck of your overwater bungalow. The more adventurous vacationers can scuba dive in some of the world's clearest oceans, swim with playful sting-rays and inquisitive whales and reef sharks, or take romantic horse rides across empty beaches. There's also deep sea fishing in waters teeming with game fish such as tuna and mahi mahi. Take a private boat charter or hop on a scooter or bicycle and ride into traditional Polynesian villages or across the quiet roads that circle French Polynesia's islands.

The overwater bungalow was invented in these very islands just over 40 years ago. Visitors have hundreds of overwater bungalows to choose from; all with their own private sunbathing decks, where couples can leap directly into the lagoon below, and at night watch the moon reflected on the water outside under a billion stars.

If you're looking for romance, you'll find it in *The Islands of Tahiti*.

Cruising & Sailing

Come Sail Away
To truly experience the awe of *The Islands of Tahiti*, nothing beats approach them from the sea. Feel the transition from the deep, untamed royal blues and rolling waves of the Pacific to the welcoming hues of a quiet, hushed lagoon. Follow the trail of flower-scented air that announces the land long before you see it. Then, watch these magical islands rise, enchanted, from the horizon. Pause to recognize the moment when you realize you're not dreaming these are *The Islands of Tahiti*.

Cruising and sailing turns to discovery in Tahitian waters where you can embark on a voyage to explore the mystical South Pacific islands and atolls. Here, the ports-of-call are uncrowded and charming, the ships are smaller and luxurious, the neon-blue waters within the lagoons are calm, and the ocean journey between the islands is short. On these voyages, each island stopover will become your next favorite idyll and unforgettable memory.

Cruises

Cruising becomes discovering in Tahitian waters where you can embark on a voyage to explore these mystical South Pacific isles. Here, the ports-of-call are uncrowded and charming, the ships are smaller and luxurious, the neon-blue waters within the lagoons are calm, and the ocean journey between the islands is short. On these voyages, each island stopover will become your next favorite idyll and unforgettable memory.

Haumana Cruises

Discovering *The Islands of Tahiti* aboard The Haumana, has something indescribable and magical. The emblematic yacht of the Polynesian lagoons, offers weekly mini-cruises of 3 nights between Bora Bora, Raiatea and Taha'a. This 12-cabin ship remains faithful to Polynesian culture and offers its passengers a true human experience in an intimate and friendly setting. On the program, sail and discover the Polynesian flavors and the various nautical and cultural activities. Proud of their culture and history, the crew members are keen to offer you all their attention to make this cruise a unique moment of sharing. With them, you will taste the Polynesian lifestyle in a preserved and friendly

www.haumana-tahiti.com

Paul Gauguin Cruises

The Paul Gauguin, historic and elegant 5 * ship, criss-crossed the Polynesian waters since 1998. Carrying its 332 passengers to inter-archipelago cruises, The Paul Gauguin has found the ideal recipe to satisfy them : Spacious and comfortable cabins, personalized service (2 crew members for 3 passengers), a cultural program with local flavors ... and an almost unlimited range of activities And many privileges. www.pgcruises.com

Wind Spirit

A sailboat is the perfect way to discover the true marvel of Tahiti. Let the trade winds inflate the sails and sail in these calm warm Polynesian waters dotted with deserted islands and characters. The Wind Spirit is a magnificent 4-masted sailboat that can accommodate 148 people. With four bridges, Wind Spirit offers its private moments rocked by a feeling of great freedom afloat. Comfort and pleasant navigation will make you forget your daily life, let yourself be guided by the Pacific Ocean!
www.windstarcruises.com

Cargo Cruises

Aranui 5

More than a means of transportation, you will live aboard an exceptional and shared adventures, learning the Polynesian lands and ancestors. As soon as you sail the Aranui 5, you will be completely immersed in Polynesian life for a 14-day adventure. This ship, baptized in December 2015, was designed to accommodate 254 passengers with 30 spacious, 40 nicely appointed standard cabins and a dormitory for 24 passengers.

www.aranui.com

Tuhaa Pae IV

Discover the Austral Islands by the sea ?

An authentic cruise aboard a freight mix (freight and passengers), reliable and comfortable. Observe the embarkation and disembarkation of the freight to these remote islands for which the Tuhaa Pae IV is a real umbilical cord. He brought food and equipment and allowed the inhabitants to export their copra and their agricultural productions to the big island.

snathp.com

Yacht Charter

Good reasons for choosing the sailing stay

Tahiti is the romantic destination, with your children, or in a group of friends, you can rent just one cabin or the whole of the boat according to the stay you dream of.

Whether you like an island rather than another, visit a pearl farm or a plantation of vanilla, a valley or a day lazing ... you are free! Free from your movements, your rhythm, your itinerary.

A professional crew You can choose to rent your boat with a crew. Or just a skipper, or a skipper and a hostess who will take care of the stewardship, the kitchen and the hygiene on board. They will be your guides, will tell you the places not to be missed ashore or on the lagoon and will be able to make you share their knowledge and experiences of the culture Polynesia

Like at the hotel! From the furnished apartment to the luxury suite, there is on a boat all the comfort of your usual holiday places and sometimes even more. The nautical charter is a floating hotel within easy reach of everyone and for everyone's enjoyment.

Sea sickness ? No swell, no pitching, no rolling on the Polynesian lagoons! Protected by the coral reef, in an incomparable setting, you slip aboard your boat as on a lake, safely.

What to do on land? Our preserved islands are full of treasures and offer several excursion possibilities. Each has its own identity, its history, its possibilities of meeting people. Visit the villages, markets, historical places, museums ... discover the coral garden, go hiking, golf or horse riding ... or enjoy a romantic evening while dining in a large hotel in Bora Bora or Taha'a

Charter Operations :
Dream Yacht Charter
www.dreamyachtcharter.com

Sunsail Yacht Charters

www.sunsail.com

Sailing Huahine Voile

www.tahitisailingcharter.com

Tahiti Yacht Charter

www.tahitiyachtcharter.com

The Moorings

www.moorings.com

Ultimate Lady

www.pacificavenues.com

Sailing in the islands

Water Activities

Floating atop the water playground of the lagoons, each ship offers unending activities for couples and families. A sample of daily activities include jetskiing, windsurfing, waterskiing, parasailing, canoeing, diving, shark feeding, and snorkeling. Hop on a glass-bottom boat to explore a lagoon or even charter your own catamaran or powerboat for the day.

Shore-side Activities

Surrounded by lush-green peaks, each island welcomes exploration by 4×4 safaris to dramatic overlooks, circle-island tours stopping off at fruit-tasting shops and historic sites, independent trips for shopping or walking through the villages, or guided hiking trips into the mountains for an overview of the land and ocean.

Unique Events

The Polynesian islands abound in sights, sounds, and experiences found nowhere else on earth and are easily discovered by cruise or yacht charter travelers. By day, live out your South Pacific fantasy when you anchor at a tiny motu for an afternoon of relaxation and fun. Or enjoy personalized tours of the historical and cultural sites hidden on each island. By night, enjoy the best Tahitian performers for elaborate and romantic displays of music and dance.

Checklist for the Perfect Sailing Experience:

- Trade winds are predictable and weak to moderate most of the year.
- Inter-island sailing is short and voyages can include multiple islands and atolls.
- Virtually every island and atoll has an 80ºF (27°C) neon-blue lagoon.

- Lagoons are calm and protected with many anchorages.

- Passes are wide, have weaker currents, and feature beacon systems.

- Supplies are easily found at island markets, marinas, shops, and food stands of fisherman and farmers.

- Safety is a part of the islands' ocean culture with a permanent VHF maritime radio channel, daily meteorological reports, emergency services and medical evacuations.

- Choices among many expert charter companies

Stopovers

The Islands of Tahiti are full of land and sea treasures. The arrival on the islands by boat, provides a real sensation of freedom, to accost like a Robinson Crusoe in search of human and cultural terrestrial discovery. Cruise by stopover is a good and a logical way to discover The Islands of Tahiti. Cruise agencies offer itineraries in the South Pacific from Papeete. For more information on foreign cruise ships, please contact the Tahiti Cruise Club Association http://www.tahiticruiseclub.com/

Here are some of the cruise companies who get to stop in The Islands of Tahiti :

- ✓ Carnival Cruises Line http://www.carnival.com/
- ✓ Celebrity Cruises http://www.celebritycruises.com/
- ✓ Costa Cruise http://www.costacruise.com/
- ✓ Cunard Cruises Line : http://www.cunardline.com.au/
- ✓ Fred Olsen ruises Line http://www.fredolsencruises.com/
- ✓ Holland America Line http://www.hollandamerica.com/main/Main.action
- ✓ Oceans Cruises : https://www.oceaniacruises.com/south-pacific-tahiti-cruises/
- ✓ Ponant cruises https://en.ponant.com/
- ✓ P&O Cruises http://www.pocruises.com/
- ✓ Royal Caribbean International http://www.royalcaribbean.fr/
- ✓ SilverSea Cruises http://www.silversea.com

Superyacht Charter

As the first hub for Superyachts in the South Pacific, *The Islands of Tahiti* offer endless cruising grounds around their 118 islands.

With 1% of land versus 99% of ocean spread over a territory as wide as the continental United States or Western Europe, both sophistication and adventure await in one of the safest places on Earth where ocean conservation has been a governmental priority for over ten years.

Cruise beautiful lagoons through the natural deep passes of the various islands, discover the friendly local people and their love for their amazing Polynesian culture, dive and snorkel world class pristine spots, enjoy the finest dining with a touch of French and Tahitian cuisine in a high end resort, indulge yourself with a local spa treatment, shop for your preferred Tahitian cultured pearls and love the barefoot luxury of a private picnic on a desert white sandy beach... *The Islands of Tahiti* have it all and will evoke even more unique emotions never experienced before.

Feel like you are a pioneer while enjoying all the comfort you would expect while cruising on a superyacht.

Local Superyacht experts will assist throughout the process of logistics and planning of your cruise whether you are chartering or sailing privately.

The Islands of Tahiti welcome an average of 50 superyachts every year. In 2016, just to name a few S/Y Vertigo, S/Y Seahawk, S/Y Destination, M/Y Askary, Fleet M/Y Vantage and AdVantage, M/Y La Dea 2, S/Y Bella Regazza, M/Y Seawolf, M/Y Suri, M/Y Senses, M/Y

Dragonfly... and a few other returning yachts will sail around French Polynesia.

Spas

With soothing lagoon waters, a rich botanical environment, air scented of vanilla and tiare flowers and the blissful tranquility of each island, *The Islands of Tahiti* offer a "spa within a spa" experience, found nowhere else on earth. Each spa in *The Islands of Tahiti* has its own unique setting from private gardens, thatched-roof open-air bungalows on the beach to overwater bungalows with tropical fish parading below, or atop hills overlooking the lagoons.

Featuring the bounty of oils, flowers and plants found only in *The Islands of Tahiti*, each spa has a full menu of treatments for couples and individuals alike.

Taurumi, the Traditional Polynesian Massage

A Polynesian massage or *taurumi* is part of the traditional medicine of the islands. It continues to be used to calm babies and in the healing arts of the *tahua* (healers). Handed down from generation to generation, *taurumi* is practiced by tracing the energy lines of the body by applying pressure with the hands and elbows. This relaxing massage, which restores both body and mind, is offered in all the spas of *The Islands of Tahiti*.

The Paradise of the Senses

Traditional Polynesian body, face, and hair treatments, manicures, body masques and wraps using local products (coconut, coffee, avocado and tropical fruit). A range of beauty secrets to leave your skin feeling soft, purified, soothed and full of freshness and luxury.

Based on the spa package you select, a relaxing massage with essential oils or hot stone completes the harmony and the serenity created by the ambience and the exclusive setting of spas designed for relaxation and intimacy. To make a romantic vacation even more romantic, the spas of *The Islands of Tahiti* provide havens of incomparable tranquillity where couples can spend an unforgettable vacation in the paradise of the senses.

Other Spa Treatments:

Spa treatments can be arranged in advance at any of these spas by your Preferred Travel Professional or through the resorts or cruise ships directly.

- Fresh-flower Bath for two
- Body wrap in a fresh banana tree leaves

- Body scrub with sand and rice, grated coconuts or sea salt
- Body wash with vanilla
- Mask with fresh fruits and plants
- Flower remedies and Aromatherapy
- Aroma Spa body treatments
- Thalassotherapy and reflexology
- Deep ocean water treatments
- Heated-stone massage
- Rain showers and rivers baths
- Full beauty care and facial

Resorts and Hotels Featuring Customized Spa Services:
Tahiti
- Hotel Tahiti Nui, Dhana Spa
- InterContinental Tahiti Resort & Spa, Deep Nature Spa by Algotherm
- Le Méridien Tahiti
- Manava Suite Resort Tahiti, Manea Spa

- Tahiti Pearl Beach Resort, TAVAI Spa by Pearl Resorts

Tetiaroa

- The Brando, Deep Nature Spa by Algotherm

Moorea

- Hilton Moorea Lagoon Resort & Spa, Moorea Lagoon Spa
- InterContinental Moorea Resort & Spa, Hélène Spa
- Manava Beach Resort & Spa Moorea, TAVAI Spa by Pearl Resorts
- Sofitel Moorea Ia Ora Beach Resort, Le Spa

Huahine

- Royal Huahine

Taha'a

- Le Taha'a Island Resort & Spa, TAVAI Spa by Pearl Resorts

Bora Bora

- Bora Bora Pearl Beach Resort & Spa
- Bora Bora Pearl Beach Resort & Spa, TAVAI Spa by Pearl Resorts
- Conrad Bora Bora Nui, Hina Spa
- Four Seasons Resort, The Spa
- InterContinental Bora Bora Resort & Thalasso Spa, Deep Ocean Spa by Algotherm

- Le Méridien Bora Bora
- Sofitel Bora Bora Marara Beach Resort, Le Spa
- Sofitel Bora Bora Private Island
- The St. Regis Bora Bora Resort, Miri Miri Spa by Clarins

Rangiroa
- Hotel Kia Ora Resort & Spa

Tikehau
- Tikehau Pearl Beach Resort, Manea Spa

Cruise
- Aranui 5
- M/S Paul Gauguin, Deep Ocean Spa by Algotherm

Golf

What's more appealing than an afternoon of golf? How about an unforgettable round of golf with the gorgeous backdrop of The Islands of Tahiti? French Polynesia offers golf fans two magnificent golf courses, one in Tahiti and another in Moorea. A mini golf is also available on Raiatea

Golf International Olivier Bréaud:

Golf International Olivier Bréaud' was created in the 1970s on an old cotton plantation on the west coast of Tahiti, at Atimaono, 41 kilometres from the centre of Papeete. It offers an 18-hole golf course that is accessible to beginners and experienced duffers alike. This course is renowned internationally for the quality of its fairways and its greens as well as for the beauty of its location. The course at Atimaono is 5,950 metres long for a 72 stroke par, and is approved by the French Golf Federation. It welcomes numerous international players annually to the Open International de Tahiti (Tahiti International Open) which today makes it part of the PGA (Professional Golf Association) FPG (Federation Polynésienne de Golf Polynesian Golf Federation) circuit.

Moorea Green Pearl:

Moorea Green Pearl is a course located in the village of Temae. The French company Grégori International created this 18 hole golf course, which was designed by the legendary American golfer Jack Nicklaus. Just a few minutes from Moorea airport (flight time from Moorea to Tahiti 10 minutes), and 10 minutes from the ferry wharf (crossing time: about half an hour), the newer of the Polynesian golf courses was inaugurated in 2007; it welcomes a growing clientele onto its 165 hectares, 650 metres of which are on the shores of the lagoon.

Mini-Golf and Practice in Raiatea:

In the south of Raiatea, in Vaiorie (PK 41, East Coast), on a lush site at the edge of the lagoon, a mini-golf of 10 holes awaits you. The low entrance fee includes the rental of clubs and balls. Clubs are available for right-handed and left-handers, for young and old alike. Reservations required to play.

Shopping

Jewellery, crafts, sarongs, monoi oil, gourmet products ... the list of souvenirs you can bring back from *The Islands of Tahiti* is endless. Our best advice? Leave lots of room for your shopping finds when you pack for your next trip. You won't regret it.

On Tahiti and the main islands frequented by tourists, you can find art galleries, *bric-à-brac*, crafts and artwork (carvings, paintings, etc.) from all the islands as well as typical Polynesian products. The Papeete market is the ideal place to to shop at the end of your stay to take home sarongs (*pareos*), baskets, works of art and a load of souvenirs. The two-story Vaima shopping centre in the centre of Papeete has a wide range of souvenirs, shops and galleries.

Hotel shops also have a large selection of souvenirs from *The Islands of Tahiti*. Local food products and cosmetics can be found in supermarkets, shops or, if you're looking for beauty products, in pharmacies. You can also buy crafts directly from producers and craftspeople during your stay.

Tahiti Cultured Pearls and Jewelry

Tahiti cultured pearls from the Tuamotu and the Gambier Islands are the must-have souvenirs for every visitor. You can buy pearls mounted or unmounted (pendants, earrings, bracelets, rings, etc.). The prices are very wide-ranging and depend on a number of criteria (quality, luster, size and shape). Strict regulation guarantees the quality of our pearls. You can request a certificate of authenticity from your reseller. Polynesian creators and designers compete to combine pearls with mother of pearl and other natural materials (wood, bone, leather, fabric, etc.) to produce original pieces.

Vanilla & Other Gourmet Grocery Products from *The Islands of Tahiti*

Tahitian vanilla is recognized as the best in the world by master chefs, who value its taste and aroma. You can find it in several forms (beans, powder, extract, etc.) by producers on our islands, in particular Taha'a, an island renowned for its high-quality vanilla plantations and beans.

Pickled mango, pineapple or papaya, fondants and fruit pastilles, honey from fragrant exotic blossoms, special vanilla, coconut and tiare flower flavored teas: Polynesian gourmet grocery products are used as the basis for a number of unique recipes just waiting for you to discover when you return home. You can find all these unique products in supermarkets and self-service stores throughout *The Islands of Tahiti*.

Monoi Oil & Cosmetics

Monoi, a term borrowed from the ancient Tahitian word *mōno'i*, is made from refined coconut oil and macerated Tahitian tiare flowers and is sold in different forms. Handmade monoi is prepared by *māmā*(grandmothers) from the islands and sold by the producers directly (along the roadside, at craft shows, etc.) and in Papeete's market. Commercially produced monoi, prepared by a number of local laboratories, is scented (sandalwood, ylang-ylang, jasmine, etc.) and can be found as a cosmetic item in supermarkets or in pharmacies (balm, creams and lotions for the body, shampoo, soap, etc.). Other local products and natural ingredients can be added to enhance its special properties (tāmanu oil, pressed from nuts with healing properties, or noni, an ancient remedy with anti-inflammatory and anti-infective properties).

The Tahiti Monoï Road is the global source of monoï oil, the famous beauty and skin oil used in cosmetics, creams and lotions. Visitors can now experience all facets of the monoï oil industry with a newly organized collective of experiences concentrated along the circle-island road. Choose from any of the 22 botanic workshops, coconut groves, tiare Tahiti flower growers, traditional and modern manufacturers, and spas that specialize in using monoï oil in their treatments. Information and maps can be provided by your Preferred Travel Professional or by your resort or cruise ship.

Carvings and Objects of Art

Marquesas islanders are experts at carving in any material (bone, wood or stone), in any size and for any use: decorative carvings, such as tiki carvings, statues, oars, clubs and puzzles, or utilitarian carvings, such as *'ūmete* (plates and bowls), *penu* (pestles), *'ana* (coconut graters), etc. *Māmās* in the Austral Islands excel in weaving and embroidery (purses, baskets, hats, mats and a variety of decorative items). The residents of the Tuamotus are experts at making all kinds of items from shells and mother-of-pearl (necklaces, vases, lampshades, a host of reproductions, etc.).

You can find these works in Papeete's art galleries on permanent or temporary display.

Sarongs (Pareos), Clothing & Accessories

The sarong, or pareo, a word derived from the Tahitian word, *pāreu*, is a piece of cloth that is usually either painted or printed with flower patterns, often dried in the sun and found in every wardrobe. Both men and women wear the pareo in any occasion, whether at home, on the beach, at parties and during traditional ceremonies and cultural events. The pareo can be knotted in several different ways and serves as more than a garment. Local artists strive to outdo each other in creativity with colors, patterns and techniques. Polynesian designers have translated pareo patterns into original ready-to-wear fashion and accessory lines such as purses, belts and shoes.

Tattoos/TĀTAU

Why not bring back an indelible souvenir to remember an unforgettable trip? Polynesian tattoo artists are known for their art and creativity. Should you decide to get one, strict hygiene requirements are enforced on all the islands.

Other Souvenirs

You can find postcards, posters, handsome photography books, calendars, key chains and other small objects for sale in souvenir and stationery stores. Postage stamps and other philatelic products are sold at Post Office branch, at the Mahina Philately Centre and online at www.tahitiphilatelie.com

Traditional Cuisine

French Polynesia benefits from fantastic weather all year round. It's a virtual Garden of Eden, where exuberance and abundance go hand in hand. In this sunny country, farmers grow a wide variety of fruits, spices and vegetables with evocative names reminding us of faraway places. These exotic treasures are much appreciated by consumers because they combine aromatic qualities with nutritional benefits, giving great pleasure to the body and the taste buds.

The legendary breadfruit plant or *'uru*, the coconut, the dozens of varieties of bananas including the incomparable orange plantain banana or *fe'i*, the various root vegetables such as the *taro*, the *tarua*, the *ufi* or even the *'umara* make up the basis of island cuisine. Papayas, mangos, pineapples, watermelon, grapefruit, limes with a pod of vanilla are used to prepare tasty deserts when dining in *The Islands of Tahiti*.

Fish from the lagoon or from the ocean, ranging from perch, *mahi mahi* and parrot fish are also on the menu for typical Polynesian dishes. They are often eaten raw, sometimes marinated in lime juice and coconut milk as in the famous recipe for 'poisson cru à la Tahitienne'.

All these tropical foods are found in traditional *ahima'a* or Polynesian ovens where fruits, vegetables, suckling pigs, Tahitian chicken *fāfā* (local spinach) and other delicacies such as *po'e* or local fruit pastilles cook through. Everything is sprinkled with fresh coconut oil and turns out deliciously creamy. There are even specialized tours that let you discover the flavors of the islands on picnics organized on beaches or on a *motu*(islet). These tours are an opportunity to taste freshly caught fish, such as the tasty *ume*, the Long Nose Emperor fish of the lagoons and the little jacks.

Tahitian Recipes

Tahitian-Style Poisson Cru *For Six People*

Ingredients

- 500g of red tuna
- 2 tomato
- 1 small cucumber
- 2 green limes
- 1 onion
- coconut milk
- parsley
- 1 green onion
- salt
- pepper

Cut the fish into small pieces and soak it in seawater or salt water for 5 minutes. In a salad bowl, put diced tomatoes and cucumbers, thinly sliced onion, cut green onion and chopped parsley. Add lemon juice, salt and pepper and let soak for a few minutes. Drain the fish, add to the bowl and mix well with other ingredients. Add the coconut milk at the last minute.

Serve immediately.

Chicken Fāfā For Six People

Ingredients

- 6 chicken breasts
- 1 bunch of *fāfā* (taro leaves)
- 2 onions
- 1 piece of ginger
- 1 lime
- 1 liter of broth
- Coconut milk

Cook the *fāfā* leaves for one hour in boiling salted water. Drain well. Cut the chicken breasts into small pieces. Peel and thinly slice the onion and ginger. Add the chicken and cook in oil for 10 minutes. Add the *fāfā* and lime juice. Mix well and let simmer for one hour. Add the coconut milk before serving.

Banana Po'e *For Six People*

Ingredients

- 6 to 8 bananas
- 150 200g of manioc, flour starch
- 50g of sugar
- Milk of a grated coconut

Peel the bananas and cook them in a little water. When they are done, drain and puree them. Mix 2 bowls of bananas with a bowl of starch and 50g of sugar. Place this mixture in a lightly oiled banana leaf. Cook in a medium hot oven for 30 to 40 minutes. Add the coconut milk just before serving.

Cooking Classes in The Islands of Tahiti

Polynesian Cooking is a blend of exotic Asian and Western flavors.

Master Chefs subtly combine fish, local produce and other local products with spices and ingredients from elsewhere. Why not try your hand in the kitchen and learn the culinary arts of *The Islands of Tahiti?* In some of the large hotels, the chef even organizes culinary workshops.

- The Chef's Workshop at Le Meridien Tahiti: An introduction to the techniques used by the chef of Le Méridien Tahiti for groups of up to 5 people. Every Tuesday and Thursday.

GREPFOC: This training institute for adults offers classes to private individuals just to delight the taste buds and to registered students to further their careers. Catering for fun ("traiteur plaisir") class. For more information, visit www.grepfoc.pf

The Islands of Tahiti

Located in the Pacific Ocean, *The Islands of Tahiti* are a mythical destination. The mention of Tahiti calls to mind visions of an idyllic island paradise and once you visit, you'll discover that your imagination isn't too off the mark. Secluded, tropical and lush, these islands are a universe where dreams meet reality.

Tuamotu Islands

Tikehau

Days evolve quietly on Tikehau. From the sky, this graceful atoll, a 55-minute flight from the kinetic bustle of Papeete in Tahiti, looks like a crown of white and pink-sand beaches shimmering around a lagoon almost too breathtaking to be true. Only about 500 Tahitians call this tranquil world home, generations of fishermen whose lives revolve around the sea. And, it's a life of both peace and plenty.

Reasons to Stay in Tikehau

A Lagoon That Keeps Its Promises

This oval shaped lagoon formed by a series of *motu* featuring white and pink sand beaches is a genuine natural pool opening to a small pass called Tuheiva. Divers are consistently enthralled by the amazing marine life where eagle rays, schools of barracudas and tuna, grey reef sharks, marine turtles and dolphins like to play. For those in search of relaxation in *The Islands of Tahiti*, Tikehau's untouched sandy beaches lying by the pure and warm emerald lagoon will definitely fill their expectations.

Natural Curiosities

Explore Tuherahera village and the superb desert atoll's beaches, see the impressive coral remnants lying on the beach on the South coast, forming a natural wall. You will travel back in time discovering the legend of Hina's bell closely linked to this place. On the *motu*, pink sand beaches, a nature's wonder, await.

A Particularly Fishy Atoll (In A Good Way!)

Millions of fish live in this untouched transparent world. The volume of fish is so much that Jacques Cousteau's research crew dubbed it "the most fish abundant Tuamotu atoll."

Manihi

Manihi conjures castaway dreams. It's as though you've arrived through a time portal into an impossible tropical fantasy. Far from the modern world, the Mana spirit of Manihi thrives around the crystal-clear lagoon that is the site of Tahiti's first black pearl farm.

Top Reasons to Stay in Manihi

Experience Our Pearl Farms
The origin of the Tahitian cultured pearl was born in Manihi in 1965. This lagoon, famous for its oyster, saw the birth of the first pearl farm. Since then, the atoll's islanders have been very passionate about producing pearls. There is a plethora of pearl farms in the lagoon of Manihi. A visit to one of these farms is a unique experience that helps you better understand exactly how much work goes into sourcing these precious gems. In *The Islands of Tahiti*, we consider pearls to be a genuine incarnation of the beauty of our Tahitian lagoons.

See A Magic Lagoon
Visitors stand in awe of Manihi's crystal clear waters and its fine sand beaches. They also enjoy snorkeling in the lagoon and drifting along Turipaoa pass. Here, fishing is too easy and kayaking is the picture-perfect experience for first-timers and seasoned travelers alike.

Get Lost In A Timeless Village

The colorful and flowery village of Turipaoa along the pass of the same name offers a peaceful Tuamotu ambience, nicely blending with the sight of basket weaving skills of local women and the sound of children splashing along the lagoon. Most houses feature a dedicated pearl farming activity. Keep an eye out for ropes, buoys and suspended mother of pearl oyster throughout Manihi.

Rangiroa

Surrounding one of the world's greatest destinations for scuba diving, the 240 islets string together in the ocean for more than 110 miles (177 km), completely encircling a deep lagoon. This is Rangiroa, a place that is simply beyond human imagination. Also the world's second largest atoll, Rangiroa is a place where land and sea form an unexpected truce. The beautiful loop of islands is surrounded by different kinds of ocean: Moana-tea (Peaceful Ocean), which defines the lagoon, and Moana-uri (Wild Ocean), where whales, manta rays, dolphins and sharks put on a show for the lucky few who come to experience their world. Back on land, the main villages of Avatoru and Tiputa offer the visitor a unique look at the South Pacific. Along the few roads that exist, you'll encounter coral churches, craft centers, local restaurants and boulangerie, along with a few tiny shops operated by locals. Wine lovers can also enjoy wine tasting at the

Dominique Auroy Estate nestled within a coconut grove, which produces three grape varieties, and black pearl farms, which dot the lagoon

Reasons to Stay in Rangiroa

A Divers' Paradise
Rangiroa is renowned worldwide for its breathtaking dive spots. Whether you take an intro dive or just a fun dive exploring the lagoon, passes and reefs, beginners and experienced divers will be blown away by the abundance and colors of the marine wildlife. Schools of multicolored butterfly fish, turtles dolphins and sharks swim just beneath the surface, just waiting for divers to visit them in their underwater paradise.

The Largest Atoll Of *The Islands Of Tahiti*
Rangiroa or Ra'iroa means "endless skies," which makes it the perfect name for the second largest atoll in the world. In fact, to give you a sense of the lagoon's scale, the inside of the lagoon is so large it could hold the entire island of Tahiti. The local people in Rangiroa mostly live on two of the hundreds of *motu* circling the atoll: Tiputa and Avatoru, close to the two passes holding the same name allowing access to the ocean.

Simply Idyllic

Even if you're not a diver, you can still discover the beauties of the lagoon from above the water's surface. The possibilities are endless on Rangiroa. You can opt to go for a picnic on a desert *motu*, go snorkeling above the incredible coral gardens, visit untouched islets where wild birds nest or, if you're feeling adventurous have fun with small, friendly sharks. A couple of must-sees include the "blue lagoon," where nature gave birth to a small lagoon within the main lagoon, as well as the "pink sand beach," another beautiful area to discover. These sand dunes emerge from the reef and naturally crushed seashells have given this amazing pink hue to the area.

Fakarava

It's easy not to notice the small, lovely islets that form a ring around the lagoon of Fakarava, the second largest atoll in French Polynesia. After all, it's the lagoon that draws your attention, its beauty pulling at you like a magnet. There is a purity in the lagoon, and in the quiet elegance of the marine life that live out their lives in the shallows near shore. It's almost as if each time you glance at it you're seeing and feeling it for the first time. Here, the world seems unblemished. Life in the small villages, with their bougainvillea lined roads, bright coral churches, quaint homes, boulangerie, snacks and restaurants seems to hover above the clear waters that surround this UNESCO Biosphere Reserve.

Top Reasons to Stay in Fakarava

It's A UNESCO Biosphere Reserve

The land and underwater wildlife in Fakarava are remarkable, including rare, endemic protected species. The atoll features such an untouched environment that it has been officially designated a UNESCO biosphere. One of the purposes of such a reserve is to combine conservation of natural resources and human development in a harmonious way (research, surveillance, training and education of locals).

It Features A Stunning Underwater World

Fakarava (meaning "beautiful" or "making things superb") is as beautiful above as it is under the water. It features fluorescent corals and divinely warm water. All you need is some simple snorkeling gear for you to fall in love with this oceanic wonder. Divers around the world dream of Fakarava: huge coral heads, schools of fish by the thousands, "walls" of sharks close to the passes … so much to experience.

"Bleu Matisse" Was Inspired Here

The famous French painter Henri Matisse (1869-1954) would claim that colors were for setting oneself free. The artist spent three months in Tahiti in 1930 exploring as far as Fakarava, where he was enthralled by the infinite variety and shades of blue of the lagoon. This discovery was such that it triggered a new creative artistic move for Matisse. Think of Fakarava visual therapy for the soul.

Other Tuamotu Islands

Featuring amazing white sand beaches lined with coconut trees, a crystal clear ocean that's warm to the touch, the 76 islands and atolls within the Tuamotu Archipelago are spread over an area of more than 700,000 sq. mi. (2 million km²). It's a land where the story of Robinson Crusoe could have actually taken place.

Living up to their reputation, the Tuamotu are a must-see for experienced divers. The atoll lagoons are a protected paradise where underwater life is spectacular. This area is also the cradle of the legendary Tahitian cultured pearl, grown with love, patience and respect, lying in a blue elegant oyster. Pearl farms lie almost weightlessly on the Tuamotu's lagoons where the pearls get their unmatched colors and shades.

Some Tuamotu atolls are just endless white, sandy beaches with a few acres of coconut plantations. Others, such as Rangiroa, the second largest atoll in the world, are much larger. These mini paradise islands, dotted idyllically amidst the aqua blue ocean, are remote yet easy to reach via boat/plane without having to go via Papeete.

You will find family pensions / guest houses around most of the islands and the largest atolls host international resorts, all welcoming visitors from around the world. Located 994 miles (1 600 km) South of Tahiti, following on from the Tuamotu atolls, emerge the most secluded and remote of *The Islands of Tahiti*: the Gambier Islands. This is a natural and cultural gem, which visitors sometimes discover by chance but from which they all come back totally seduced.

Takapoto

Idyllic and pristine, the Takapoto atoll is a dream paradise. Discovered by French explorers Jacques Lemaire and Willem Schouten, Takapoto is a closed island without a real pass allowing the lagoon and ocean to meet. This is the reason why the atoll has remained so untouched. It is also the home of the famous black pearl (from the oyster *Pinctada margaritifera*), the main resource on the island. Visitors will enjoy seeing the numerous fish parks made out of coral stones.

Anaa

The coral ring of Anaa is still easily recognized by Polynesian sailors thanks to the bright emerald color of its lagoon. The atoll doesn't have a pass and shelters spectacular *feo*, huge 10-foot high coral blocks emerging from the lagoon.

Mataiva

Located at the northwest end of the Tuamotu Archipelago, Mataiva is a surprising small atoll. It is the only lagoon of French Polynesia to feature 70 interior pools approximately 26 feet deep with nine channels. This is where the name "the island of nine eyes" originates. A real-life tropical aquarium, snorkelers and other visitors will marvel at the beautiful fish-filled lagoon.

Hao

Discovered by Pedro Fernández de Quirós in 1606, Hao, still called "Bow Island" or "Harp Island" given its shape, features one of the largest lagoons in French Polynesia. Open to the ocean via Kaki pass, the immense lagoon is an underwater mass hiding unknown treasures for divers to discover. Starfish, sea urchins and crustaceans are only a few of the inhabitants of the coral reef, which is also visited by mahi-mahi and silver jackfish.

Makemo

Makemo is a work of art carved by the nature of erosion over a period of thousands of years. The sand is an amazing blend of pink and red due to micro-organisms developing in these warm shallow waters.

A few steps from the shore lies a marvelous natural pool welcoming swimmers into clear, turquoise waters. This is truly an idyllic place where dreams and legends meet, its messages still transmitted by the ancient guardians of the island's history.

Ahe

Located between Rangiroa and Manihi, Ahe atoll is a place for visitors seeking authenticity. Dotted with picturesque pearl farms, this is one of the most dynamic atolls in *The Islands of Tahiti*. Visit a pearl farm and learn all the secrets of this amazing activity while discovering the passion and respect the islanders have for this heavenly, but fragile environment.

Reao

You have arrived at the edge of the world. Reao is far away from everything, lost and untouched. The island itself discouraged the most reckless navigators of history. The French navigator Louis Isidore Duperray was the first to go through the cape in 1823, naming it "Clermont-Tonnerre."

Kauehi

Well known to pearl merchants in the 19th Century, this atoll was first mentioned in the writings of British captain Robert FitzRoy in 1835. Between 1838 and 1842, the American expedition led by Charles Wilkes named the island "Vincennes" after his ship.

Aratika

Aratika is located 301 miles northeast of Tahiti and 31 miles (21 km) from Fakarava which has administrative authority on the island. Just like Fakarava, the atoll is part of a UNESCO biosphere thanks to its exceptional natural and cultural heritage.

Arutua

Arutua is a ring-shaped island also known as Ngaru-atua, which means "breaking wave coming from afar", it is located 18 nautical miles east of Rangiroa. The atoll comprises some fifty *motu* encircling a huge lagoon with one islet at the center. The village, Rautini, is where most of the population of Arutua live. Many fish farms dot the lagoon. Fishing, pearl farming and copra farming account for the income of most Arutua people.

Society Islands

From the country's main island, Tahiti, across to her enchanting sister island, Moorea, then up to Marlon Brando's Tetiaroa paradise atoll, these Windward Islands are tropical dream islands! Choose between the various land/water activities or just relax by the pool. There is something for everyone in *The Islands of Tahiti*

Tahiti

Crowned by a circle of majestic peaks, Tahiti, the largest island in French Polynesia, towers over the ocean like a proud and royal Queen. The mountainous interior is adorned with mystical valleys, clear streams, and high waterfalls. Most of the island's population resides near the shore, leaving the interior of the island feeling almost untouched and ancient, despite such proximity to the bustling capital of Papeete. Papeete, meaning "water basket," was once a gathering place where Tahitians came to fill their calabashes with fresh water. Now, Papeete, the touchstone of this island nation, boasts world-class resorts, spas, fine dining and unique restaurants, nightclubs, vibrant markets, museums, pearl shops, and boutiques.

Tahiti... Just the word...

The world's definition of paradise.

Reasons to Stay in Tahiti

A Lively Culture

The largest and most lively of *The Islands of Tahiti*, known simply as Tahiti, lives at the pace of culture, music and dance. Attend an enchanting Tahitian dance show called *'ori* Tahiti, or visit a contemporary art exhibition, an unusual play, a traditional or modern concert. Tahiti and especially Papeete provide the opportunity to discover artistic expression of all kinds.

An Authentic Experience

Tahiti is also famous for its hospitality and sweet, relaxed atmosphere where everyone is welcome. The first thing visitors will notice is that the spontaneous and sincere friendliness of Tahitians is hard to match. Here, people smile all the time and often take the time to share a piece of advice, information or a story. Visitors will instantly feel comfortable living at the pace of island life.

Nature + Activities

As you travel throughout the islands, Tahiti slowly unveils its beauty. It can be explored in many different ways: black sand beaches on the East coast, white sand beaches on the West coast, diving, beginner's and legendary surf spots, mountainous peaks within desert lush valleys or the historic site of Papeete's colorful market and, oh, so much more.

Moorea

Moorea rises magically out of the ocean like a cathedral. High, sharp, inspiring green spires, crowned by clouds. Poetic threads of waterfalls tumble down fern-softened cliffs. Peaceful meadows flanked by pinnacles of emerald green will renew your belief in the majesty of nature, and Moorea's bright blue lagoon will bring to life the South Seas idyll of your dreams. Pastel-painted houses, surrounded by gardens of hibiscus and birds of paradise, circle the island in a necklace of happy, simple villages that will elevate your senses and remind you that this is what life is all about. *La vie heureuse,* as they say in Tahiti, a happy life. One of the most memorable locations in *The Islands of Tahiti*, Moorea's beauty is unforgettable.

Reasons to Stay in Moorea

It's A Natural Playground

The quiet waters of the lagoon and the annual trade winds from April to October allow for a variety of activities, from outrigger canoeing to paddle boarding, kite boarding, water skiing and even surfing around of some of the passes. One of *The Islands of Tahiti*, Moorea is a haven for divers who instantly fall in love with the varied coral reef eco-system and the colorful mix of marine life. While scuba diving or snorkeling, you might encounter stingrays, sharks and marine turtles in a clear lagoon sparkling with different shades of blue. On the mountain side, the sharp landscape is watched over by eight summits featuring a magnificent ancient volcanic crater which has now become a lush valley. It is the perfect area for hiking, horseback riding, quad biking or exploring on a four-wheeler.

Polynesian Charm and Ambiance
Colorful, flowered and radiant, the island of Moorea is a pleasure for all the senses. Stroll luxuriously between gardens and white sand beaches, myriad flowers and pineapple plantations or watch fishermen on their outrigger canoe or to listen to the sound of the *'ukulele* sitting under a *purau* tree *(Hibiscus tiliaceus)*. You'll relish these magical moments and this unmatched world of enchantment.

A Source of Inspiration
Many artists live on the island of Moorea. Painters, carvers, jewelers and tatoo artists have settled down on this island and take their time to capture the island's beauty and serenity and find the inspiration to create their art.

Raiatea

The heartbeat of *The Islands of Tahiti* emanates from a special place in Raiatea, the sacred Taputapuatea *marae*. The expansion of Polynesians throughout the Pacific began on Raiatea from this exact site. After offering blessings through sacred ceremonies and celebrations, outriggers with original settlers ventured north to Hawaii and west to New Zealand. Raiatea, meaning "faraway heaven" and "sky with soft light," was first named Havai'i as is considered the homeland of the ancient Polynesians. Recognized as the most sacred island in the region, the green-carpeted mountains rise to the cloud-capped peak of the celebrated Mt. Temehani.

Learn more about Raiatea and *The Islands of Tahiti's* cultural history here

Reasons to Stay in Raiatea
The Cradle of Polynesian Culture
Formerly named Hava'i, Raiatea is known as the gods' cradle, hosting archeological treasures (*marae*, petroglyphs…) and eons of history and culture. As the first Polynesian island to be populated, Raiatea shelters the most spectacular and first international *marae* of the Polynesian triangle, called Taputapuatea. This is where inauguration ceremonies, political alliances and international meetings would take place in ancient times. The site was taboo and was the headquarters of religious and political powers of the Polynesian region. These days, communities of Hawaii, New Zealand and Cook Islands still meet at this pilgrimage venue, which they consider as the home of their sacred culture.

A Sailing Paradise

Raiatea is the top yachting location in *The Islands of Tahiti*. Most charter companies and marinas have chosen to settle around Raiatea. The island hosts a large number of moorings, bays (deep and calm) in a pristine and amazing environment (volcano craters, waterfalls). The sailing conditions are excellent. It is a pleasure cruising to the other peaceful Leeward Islands, all as beautiful inside or outside the lagoon.

A Unique Natural Heritage
Raiatea is an incredible natural source of interest for scientists and nature lovers due to its rare flora and fauna species. Mount Temehani shelters the *tiare 'apetahi* (and about 30 other endemic plants), a flower found nowhere else in the world. It has become the symbol for Raiatea. This half-circle white and delicate flower only blooms at dawn.

Raiatea also shelters the only navigable river in French Polynesia. Go on an unusual outrigger canoe ride in the heart of a dense tropical forest of *purau*, bamboos and *māpē* (*Inocarpus fagiferus*). Legend says that the river would have been the departure point of all Polynesian migrations to Hawaii and New Zealand.

Bora Bora

Romance. It rises from the velvet blues of the deep water up through the softer hues of the lagoon and into the air that surrounds Bora

Bora. Its touch on the sea breeze tingles the skin. And its power fills each beat of the heart. A brief 50-minute flight from The Islands of Tahiti or Moorea, Bora Bora, with a lagoon resembling an artist's palette of bright blues and greens, is love at first sight. Romantics from around the world celebrate this island where the lush tropical slopes and valleys of Mount Otemanu blossom with hibiscus, while palm-covered motu circle the illuminated lagoon like a delicate necklace.

Perfect white-sand beaches give way to azure waters where tropical-colored fish animate the coral gardens and giant manta rays glide leisurely past. This could easily be defined as the center of the romantic universe, where luxury resorts and spas dot the island with overwater bungalows, thatched-roof villas and a fabled ambience. Simply put, Bora Bora is one of the most beautiful islands in the world.

Top Reasons to Stay in Bora Bora

A Stunning Lagoon
Bora Bora is a volcano set on one of the most beautiful lagoons in the world, a million shades of blue. The huge *motu* of Bora Bora's white sand beaches lined with coconut trees encircle the emerald lagoon populated with myriad fish and multi-colored corals.

An Overwater Paradise

A peaceful haven sitting directly over the lagoon, the overwater bungalow concept is a can't-miss element of Bora Bora and *The Islands of Tahiti*. From rooms, suites of floating villas, lose yourself in the colors of the lagoon framed by unforgettable sunsets. Designed and built in traditional Tahitian style, these bungalows offer direct access to the lagoon and are the perfect relaxing getaway.

So Many Activities
Bora Bora's lagoon is an underwater world that hosts manta rays, sharks and gentle Napoleon wrasses, which will welcome you while scuba diving, helmet diving or viewing from a glass-bottom boat. There are many opportunities to explore the lagoon, the *motu* and the ocean. Options include but aren't limited to fishing, cruises, jet ski, kite boarding, paddle boarding, outrigger canoe rides and more. And, don't forget about taking a four-wheeler, going for a hike or taking it all in from the air in an unforgettable helicopter tour.

Maupiti

There are places in *The Islands of Tahiti* where you can indulge in five-star, brand name resorts, and there are places where you can immerse yourself into the ebb and flow of daily life, experiencing this island nation like a local. If you're looking for a place where the brand names are sand, sea, sun, time and tide, the Maupiti will wrap you in her arms and gently indulge you like a member of the family.

Located 195 miles (315 km) northwest of the island of Tahiti and 25 miles (40 km) West of Bora Bora, Maupiti is a tiny island (7 miles / 11 square kilometers), secluded and authentic. Whether you fly from Papeete or take the boat from Bora Bora, Maupiti will immediately seduce with its splendor and quiet pace of life. Magnificent sceneries, endless white sandy beaches both on the island and the motu, legendary rocky peaks and ancient *marae* all blend nicely with the friendly and smiling style of the islanders.

Reasons to Stay in Maupiti

A Small, Picturesque Island

The unmatched charm of Maupiti is reflected in every inhabitant and family guesthouses where you will be introduced to the Tahitian lifestyle. Here, people mostly travel riding a bicycle or a canoe, which are marvelous ways to take your time and explore the beauties of the island. Stroll along the little road circling Maupiti or in the heart of the lagoon and enjoy every single moment of your time in *The Islands of Tahiti*.

Cultural Wealth

There are still important *marae* on Maupiti: Vaiahu, Ofera, pre-European sites loaded with history. Petroglyphs were carved on huge rocks in Haranae valley while the legendary outrigger canoe of the demigod and hero, Hiro, lies in Vaitia valley. Just like anywhere else around *The Islands of Tahiti*, the combination of nature and mythical stories is extremely powerful here.

Unusual Discoveries
Climbing up Mount Teurafaatiu (elevation 1,250 ft. / 381 m.) offers an amazing panoramic view. The 360-degree view on the lagoon, *motu* and shape of Bora Bora in the distance is unforgettable. From Tereia beach, superb and picturesque, you will walk to Motu Auria across, joined by stingrays. Cliffs, caves and other local discoveries await visitors.

Tetiaroa

Some places you can feel. They cast their spell on you immediately. This is Tetiaroa. A haven for birds, sea turtles and all kinds of marine life, Tetiaroa is treasured among Tahitians who know it as a sacred place. So sacred, that at one time the coconut-dotted white sand beaches and crystalline lagoon of this uninhabited atoll was an exclusive getaway for Tahitian royalty. It's not surprising that actor Marlon Brando fell under its spell during the filming of "Mutiny on the Bounty" in 1960, and later went on to become its owner. Now you can follow in the wake of kings and Hollywood royalty with a quick 15-minute private charter from Tahiti or Moorea.

Among the islets, Tahuna Iti, the Birds' Island, is a national reserve for sea birds, frigates, sterns, phaetons (straw tails), brown gannets and other petrels

Reasons to Stay in Tetiaroa

An Unforgettable Atoll, A Stone's Throw Away From Tahiti

With limited ways to get to this island, the best method is to join a weekend cruise departing from Papeete to access this fragile but preserved island, which serves as a bird sanctuary. The island is looking to be granted a special status of natural reserve in order to regulate access and promote best practices for a sustainable and responsible approach of excursions.

A Bird Sanctuary

Tetiaroa shelters one of the largest colony of birds in Tahiti. White terns, brown boobies, frigate birds, red-tailed tropic birds and the amazing great crested birds whose colony is the only one in the Windward Islands all coexist in Tetiaroa. Birds come to breed in this uninhabited haven and their environment has to be respected and preserved in all possible ways.

The Brando: A New High-End Eco-Hotel

Launched in 2014 on Motu Onetahi, the Brando is setting new standards for luxury accommodations in *The Islands of Tahiti*. It is unique in all respects and relies entirely on renewable energy with solar panels and coconut oil. Sea water air conditioning (SWAC) is a key element by producing cold air with ocean water from 3,150 ft. deep (960 meters). Nearly invisible from the sea, the 35 villas are beautifully integrated with the magnificent landscape. A scientific research eco-station is contributing to the research, conversation and education related to Tetiaroa and its amazing biodiversity. A desalination plant will provide the resort with fresh water, while rain water is collected from the technical area buildings. The resort is confident that it will soon obtain LEED platinum certification, the highest accolade of this most respected program for assessing the environmental impact of new constructions. The other islets remain undeveloped and are serving as field for scientific observation and data collection.

Huahine

Huahine casts a spell over you from the moment you arrive. Only a 40-minute flight from the island of Tahiti, the enchanted Huahine, with its lush forests, untamed landscape and quaint villages, is one of Tahiti's best-kept secrets, a place where you can live like a local. A deep, crystal-clear lagoon surrounds the two islands that comprise Huahine, while magnificent bays and white-sand beaches add drama to the experience. Relatively unchanged by the modern world, Huahine offers the slower, more tranquil pace of old Polynesia. With only eight small villages scattered across the island, the few residents welcome visitors with great kindness. Not surprisingly, this fertile world offers a rich soil providing the local farmers a bountiful harvest of vanilla, melons and bananas.

Top Reasons to Stay in Huahine

Charm Meets Seclusion
Also commonly referred to as the "secret island," the "authentic island" and the "secluded island," many charming adjectives come to mind when mentioning Huahine, and for obvious reasons. The island is a delicious cocktail of Polynesian sceneries and ambiance. Find natural beauty, experience intense encounters with the population, explore the infinite possibilities for adventure and relaxation, alike. Huahine is an island "to live," an island "to feel." The famous local singer and painter Bobby Holcomb has chosen this small piece of land where joy and smiles are always around.

Cultural Discoveries
Maeva, North-East of Fare, is located close to the largest of the two lagoons, called Fa'una Nui. It is famous for its farming activities.

Stonefish traps an ancestral legacy that's still used along with numerous *marae* and other archeological remnants are concentrated around this authentic village. A small educational museum was set up under a *fare pōte'e* (a house where the local knowledge, sacred traditions and rituals were taught) to exhibit objects and other remnants found during the various archeological digs (paddles, axe blades, fish teeth pendants, pestles, tattoo combs....). In Faie, get close to the huge blue eyed eels.

Activities for Everyone
Beautiful white sand beaches lie in the districts of Fare and Parea. Go on a lagoon ride on the unreal colored lagoon, explore the underwater world (reef walls, fishy caves and coral gardens) and one of the largest archeological areas of *The Islands of Tahiti*, enjoy a sunset cruise, deep-sea fishing, surfing, hiking, horseback riding, trekking and kite boarding. Water and land activities abound around the island.

Taha'a

Life slows on the island of Taha'a in *The Islands of Tahiti*. This quiet island will sweep you away into the traditional, tranquil life of the Tahitians. The flower-shaped island's simple beauty comes in soft mountains, surrounded by tiny *motu* with bright, white-sand beaches. Vanilla-scented air wafts on breezes that flow down the hillsides from numerous vanilla farms, and these soft aromas ride the ocean breezes announcing the soul of the island long before you even see it on the horizon

Reasons to Stay in Taha'a

The Authentic Charm of the Island
Time seems to have stopped in Taha'a, a secretive and secluded island. While strolling along paths across the island, travelers will discover unspoiled vegetation.

Vanilla Discovery
Discovering the secrets of vanilla in its natural environment will make you fall in love with Taha'a even more. Visitors enjoy sampling *vanilla tahitensis*, a unique and precious vanilla that tastes like paradise. A certain artistic know-how is required to grow this exquisite spice. It's a skill that's acquired over time and with great experience. Just like patient alchemists, specialists pamper their vanilla for many months before the miracle begins to happen.

A Big Fish Tank
Feel like Robinson Crusoe, lying on the fine sand dotted with beautiful palm trees, facing crystal clear water on the *motu* of Taha'a. The scenery is perfect in and out of the water. Snorkelers will find many coral heads in this rich underwater world.

Tupai

What if the most romantic atoll in the world was heart-shaped and located just a few short miles from Bora Bora? Welcome to the island of "Pere," goddess of fire and passion, a place so untouched and pristine that visiting it is a privilege.

Located 10 miles North of Bora Bora, the islet of Tupai, viewed from the sky, features a heart. It hosts a double lagoon and *motu* covered with coconut trees. Many birds have chosen to live on the island and sea turtles lay their eggs on the beach from November onward.

Tupai has no residents and, therefore, no accommodations. But, if you're up for a few hours on a romantic, deserted island, you can take a short visit to raise a glass of champagne or celebrate your wedding surrounded by breathtaking scenery.

Gambier Islands

Located more than 994 miles (1,600 km) southeast of the island of Tahiti and at the end of the Tuamotus, this archipelago is the most remote and also the least populated region of French Polynesia. Counting only 1,000 inhabitants, it shelters four mountainous islands lying within the same lagoon: Mangareva, 'Akamaru, 'Aukena and Taravai, with dozens of islets, called motu

Mangareva

The remote Gambier Islands lie just a little more than 1,000 miles (1,600 kilometers) southeast of Tahiti. Polynesian mythology tells of Mangareva being lifted from the ocean floor by the demi-god Maui. The mountains of Mangareva rise over the surrounding islands and the luminous lagoon like a great cathedral. Although once the center for Catholicism in Polynesia, the people of Mangareva have returned to a more traditional Polynesian lifestyle and the island has become an important supply source for the Tahitian cultured pearl industry. Along with the pearl farms and tours of the island by road or boat, travelers can also explore the surprising number of surviving churches, convents, watchtowers and schools from the 1800s. Some structures are still in use such as St. Michel of Rikitea Church where the altar is inlaid with iridescent mother-of-pearl shell

Reasons to Stay in Mangareva

A Secluded Group of Islands
The Gambier archipelago is well off the beaten track. Travelers visiting this area will feel a sense of privilege as they're greeted warmly by locals. The islands are still secluded and offer natural and cultural treasures, which creates a perfect mix of well-being and a unique change of scenery.

A Breathtaking Lagoon & Lush Mountains

The lagoon, hosting the entire archipelago, is probably the most beautiful of *The Islands of Tahiti*. Both transparent and sandy, turquoise and dotted with coral heads, it displays a range of blues marvelously contrasting with the surrounding lush green mountains. Hikers will find endless treasures while exploring Mangareva.

The Largest Cathedral In French Polynesia
Although Mangareva hosts some pre-European remnants of *marae* and other artifacts, Mangareva is renowned for its fascinating religious 19th Century heritage. They say faith can move mountains. In Gambier, it has moved tons of coral. As the cradle of Catholicism in Polynesia, Gambier features hundreds of religious buildings built by missionaries and islanders alike between 1840-70. These include churches, presbyteries, convents, schools and observation towers. You can visit them in Rikitea, 'Akamaru, 'Aukena and Taravai. Some of them are remarkably preserved while others are in ruins. The largest and oldest monument of French Polynesia proudly stands in Rikitea. Cathedral Saint Michel (1848) Was most recently renovated in 2012.

Marquesas Islands

Legendary high cliffs, volcanic peaks, impressive remnants wrapped in wild nature, amazing beaches: the Marquesas are breathtaking. Located 932 miles (1,500km) away from Papeete, they offer the traveler a trip of a lifetime. The Marquesans call their islands "Land of Men," or "Te Henua 'Enana."

Marquesas Islands

Golden rays of light filter through the clouds suspended on sharp mountainous peaks, drawing an unreal and subtle ambience. Lush and high islands emerge from the Pacific Ocean, a land of history and legend, all as fascinating as unforgettable. Welcome to "The Land of Men," the Marquesas Islands. The Marquesas are located 932 miles (1,500 km) northeast of Tahiti and spread out over 12 islands, of which only six are inhabited.

Reasons to Stay in the Marquesas Islands

A Show of Culture & Nature

Framed by looming cliffs, the coasts of the Marquesas Islands are a mix of black sand beaches and gorgeous bays. In the lush rainforest, where thousands of pre-European remnants lie, you'll discover wild horses, goats and bores. Nature is raw and its charm even stronger. From Taipivai Valley to Hatiheu Bay, from Anaho to Hakaui (Vaipo, the highest waterfall in *The Islands of Tahiti*), the traveler is invited to admire cultural and natural wonders. The Marquesans are said to be among the finest craftsmen throughout French Polynesia. They create large and fine carvings, beautiful tattoos, surprising pieces of jewelry.

Following Melville's Track in Taipivai Valley

This is the story of a sailor who was attempting to flee a boat, a boat he detested. He secretly disembarked on a hard, impenetrable island. He wandered around alone but was soon welcomed by the Taipi clan. However he was afraid they were cannibals. Not only did they treat him well (nor eat him!) but they also allowed him as the first European ever to discover their unknown and untouched community. It was in 1842. Today, following his steps is a mystical pilgrimage as the valley hosts hundreds of remnants such as tiki and petroglyphs in a timeless atmosphere.

Incredible Dives
Although Nuku Hiva is not thought to be a great scuba diving destination, it is, in fact, quite thrilling. The geographical isolation of the island has allowed a phenomenal biodiversity to develop. In the open ocean, encounter an abundance of manta rays, eagle rays, sharks of various species and sizes, jackfish, tuna, dolphins and swordfish. A pod of several hundred melon-head dolphins live close to the coast and can often be seen.

Gauguin and Brel's Memories
In 1901, Paul Gauguin and later in 1975, Jacques Brel, both came to Hiva Oa in quest of what could be referred to as personal inner peace. While we don't know if they ever found it, every morning, as the sun rises, the light over the island is breathtakingly pure, so pure that you

feel like you're part of eternity. This is an unspeakable feeling that every traveler will experience. Walking these same artistic footsteps includes visiting their graves at the Calvaire cemetery where they both rest facing Taaoa's Bay under the sweet fragrance of frangipani trees. Then, visit the replica of Gaugin's "Maison du Jouir" and the small museum dedicated to the painter and his house. While he lived in the Marquesas, he painted some of his most famous artwork, sourcing his inspiration through the islanders' every day life but also legends and old religious traditions representing imaginary scenes.

Tiki Island
Hiva Oa is worth visiting for its various archeological sites such as *me'ae* in Puama'u, hosting the largest tiki statue of *The Islands of Tahiti*. "Takaii" (8 feet / 2.4 meters) is a one-of-a-kind smiling statue, hidden in lush vegetation. Petroglyphs, such as the female travel Chief's polished stone mirror, are in the surrounding area. Taaoa is home to a huge cult area featuring lithic structures and tiki statues nicely blending within the untouched and primitive nature around them: giant banyan trees, breadfruit trees, coconut and papaya trees.

Endless Hiking & Riding Opportunities
Whether you go hiking, horseback riding or on a 4WD ride, explore the pristine and breathtaking landscapes of Hiva Oa featuring waterfalls,

peaks, fording and crossing rivers. It's 123 square miles of enjoyment for nature lovers.

The Marquesas Islands

Nuku Hiva
If God had a "big house" symbolizing the Marquesas Islands, the largest of them Nuku Hiva would represent the top of the framework. The vertiginous volcanic peaks and amazing slopes blend with the blue of the Pacific Ocean. A special universe opens its doors. The starting point of your adventure is Taioha'e, the archipelago's regional capital, opening at the end of a large bay holding the same name. outstanding landscapes, an incredible archeological history, great stories and a rich culture are all to be discovered alongside a friendly population.

Hiva Oa
According to legend, Hiva oa is the main beam of Gods' "big house." Today, it is commonly named the "Garden of the Marquesas" thanks to its fertile and lush land. The island features endless untouched nature: green, invading and bright. Roads and houses are rarely seen. The island's rugged landscapes blend sharp ridges, peaks and valleys scattered with archeological sites and ruins. They are home to the largest tiki statues of French Polynesia. Hiva oa is lined with black sand beaches and sharp cliffs diving into the Pacific Ocean.

The island's main village, Atuona, is nested at the end of Taaao Bay and is overlooked by the highest mountains (Mount Temetiu 4,186 ft. and Mount fe'ani 3,366 ft.). This is also the place where two famous artists chose to live their lives: the french painter Paul Gaugin and the French poet, singer and actor Jacques Brel.

Ua Pou
Ua pou symbolizes the entrance pillars to God's house. Huge basaltic columns reaching the sky and holding the names of legendary warriors: Poutetaunui and Poumaka. In 1888, they inspired poet Robert Louis Stevenson, who mentioned them as "volcanic arrows looking like a church bell tower." They proudly overlook the bay of Hakahau village, the main village on the island.

Ua Huka
Ua Huka symbolizes the "food basket" at God's house and features more untouched beauty and is renowned for its dry soil and landscapes. Wild horses gallop as far as the eye can see around this desert-colored land. Goats climb up on the island's high plains. Peaceful and mystical, Ua Huka invites the traveler to discover a secluded universe, where the island's ancestors are not just a part of the past but still very much part of the islanders' everyday life.

Tahuata

Tahuata symbolizes "sunrise" or "the enlightening home" at God's house: a poetic image expressing reality so well. Small, Tahuata's only access is by sea from Hiva oa. The island offers charming discoveries to the privileged traveler. From its fertile valleys to its crystal clear bays, Tahuata is an exquisite haven of peace, a place of history and creativity. Most inhabitants make a living out of their remarkable fine artwork, such as bone and rosewood or miro (Thespesia populnea) carving. Mono'i is made following the scents of traditions and secrets, like an invite to a mesmerizing perfume beautifully named "love potion" by the islanders.

Fatu Hiva
Fatu Hiva symbolizes the roof of Gods' house: a small but stunning island. Arriving by sea, you're greeted by sheer landscapes and pristine vegetation. Fatu Hiva will mesmerize visitors. In 1937, Thor Heyerdahl and his wife, in quest of a genuine return to nature, set foot on the island to live like at the dawn of the new world. Not much has changed. Today, most local people live around the village of Omoa where they make traditional and renowned tapa out of tree bark. Hanavave is sheltered within an amazing bay: the Bay of the Virgins, probably one of the most beautiful bays on Earth, especially at dusk when the light blazes the volcanic peaks turning the landscape into an unreal and unforgettable scene.

Austral Islands

As their name implies, the Austral islands, located south of The Island of Tahiti, on the Tropic of Capricorn, represent the southernmost boundary of French Polynesia. The climate is cooler than in Tahiti and the shape and ecology of these self-sufficient islands make them a charming world apart

Austral Islands
Discovered by Europeans in the 18th Century, the Australs are located 373 miles (600 km) south of Tahiti's capital city. The archipelago is made of seven islands, five of which are inhabited and four of which are accessible by air. An untouched and mysterious land where white sand clashes with the intense blue of the lagoons, the Australs are off the beaten track, offering a memorable and unique experience in *The Islands of Tahiti.*

Breathtaking landscapes, from sheer mountains to valleys and high plains, these islands are famous for their farming activities. Quite a few archeological remnants hide on each island, bearing witness to a well organized pre-European community of rich cultural and religious practices.

The cliffs and caves of the Austral Islands are places of legends. These areas used to be old burial grounds but are now a place to watch humpback whales frolic in the waters just offshore. The whales come to the Austral Islands from August to October each year to give birth.

These contrasting sceneries blend well with the friendliness of the inhabitants. Visit colorful, picturesque villages to discover the handiwork of islanders who mainly live off their artwork. Also enjoy watching fishermen, farmers and basket weavers at work. You're not likely to leave without a hat or woven basket to remind you of your magical time in the Austral Islands.

The Austral Islands are a rare opportunity to discover *The Islands of Tahiti* in a different light.

Top Reasons to Visit the Austral Islands

Whale Watching: Humpback whales arrive in Rurutu each year. They come between August and October to mate and give birth in Rurutu's amazingly clear waters. Mothers and calves swim under the water while males and females communicate offering whale watchers a moment of pure bliss.

Unknown Archeological Remnants: Numerous Pre-European archaeological remnants can still be found around Tubuai. Most of them hide abandoned behind lush vegetation, but some of them are well looked after and are worth a visit. Please ask a professional guide or your hosts in order to visit these ruins. Your guides will tell you the stories of the *marae* and the island's legends in a unique authentic way.

Raw Nature: The island is a great mix of beautiful white fine sand, deserted beaches, a crystal clear lagoon, lush valleys and varied farming, majestic peaks and hiking trails. Land and sea blend nicely to provide travelers with a enough experiences to complete a bucket list.

The Austral Islands

Rurutu: The island was formed by a pair of consecutive volcanic hot spots, which created unusual mountains circled with coral cliffs. This natural occurrence led to the island's "Rurutu," or, "the gushing rock." Basaltic rocks and a limestone belt offer surprising stalactites and stalagmites around the former lagoon, now a coral reef.

The cool climate leads to lush vegetation covering the island's rocks. The curvy road will lead you through a poetic and impressive tour, combining long, white sandy beaches, beautiful bays and various plantations. Coffee, pineapple, wild basil and lychees abound around these rich lands.

Within this pristine environment, just 2,404 inhabitants look after their traditions and organize friendly games. The feast of Tere or island tour gathers all villages and allows the strongest to lift volcanic rocks as heavy as 330 pounds (150 kg).

You can best discover the charms of Rurutu by interacting with the local people, such as the mamas, smiling ladies who spend their days weaving specialty materials. Their agile hands make delicate artwork such as *pe'ue* or mats and also fine woven hats. They are also experts in the making of *tifaifai*, traditional patchwork blankets featuring exotic patterns and requiring patience and knowhow.

Finally, do not miss a whale water ballet, attracting nature and whale lovers and researchers each year. Whales come very close to the coast to give birth, and adventurous snorkelers can share a very special moment with these sea giants.

Tubuai: Tubuai is the largest island of this archipelago and hosts the main public and economic services for this island group. Its reef is scattered with fine *motu* plus coral and volcanic rocks. The huge lagoon, nearly twice as large as the island itself, offers 33 sq. mi. (85 km²) of pure aquatic fun. The mild climate also makes these islands ideal for farming. Lilies are grown around the islands for export and can be seen in the fields as far as the eye can see.

The first explorers were struck by the island's beauty. Toward the end of the 19th Century, explorers Wallis and Cook took a liking to the lush vegetation and crystal clear water of the island. However, the area did not look appropriate for good anchorage given the large barrier reef around the coast. This disadvantage turned into an incredible advantage in the eyes of the famous mutineers of the HMS Bounty. Led by Christian Fletcher, they tried unsuccessfully to settle and built Fort George, which no longer exists.

Raivavae: The island features a large lagoon circled by a coral reef consisting of 28 *motu*. The cool climate allows for agriculture. The inhabitants, living in four different villages, grow taro and coffee but also mango and banana trees.

"Raivavae" or "the open sky" is a great place to listen to the sounds of sea bird songs, the swell of the ocean and the gentle wind. Often considered the most beautiful island of the Pacific, the magnificent scenery of Raivavae lives up to its reputation as the Garden of Eden. Floating over an emerald lagoon, the island shelters amazing remnants from the past such as a laughing tiki. Numerous items are kept in private collections at Western museums from an era that witnessed intense pre-European religious and cultural practices.

Locals have chosen to keep their island untouched and have developed an ecotourism concept welcoming travelers in a warm and simple manner. Aside from handicrafts, Raivavae is the only island where sewn outriggers are still made, ensuring the visitor a step back in time feeling while on the island.

Rimatara: Although Rimatara is the smallest island of the Austral archipelago, it holds a particular charm with many hidden beauties. Around this circle shaped island, it feels as though time has stopped. With just a small lagoon, the island is also one of the last shelters for an endangered bird species, the *khul's lorikeet* or *vini 'ura*, a bird whose colorful feathers brighten up Rimatara's sky. Access to the island was by sea until recently. Now you you can now fly from Papeete.

The main occupation of the population, aside from farming, is basket weaving and especially the preparation of *fara pae'ore* leaves (a variety of thornless pandanus) used as a material to make woven items.

Plan your Trip Before you go

Transportation

The Tahiti-Faa'a international airport, built on the lagoon, is about 5 km west of Papeete near several major hotels.
The domestic terminal for Air Tahiti is located right inside. The airport provides a lot of other functions and related services.

Where are The Islands of Tahiti ?

The Islands of Tahiti are located equidistant south of the equator as Hawaii is north, in the same time zone as Hawaii, and halfway between California and Australia.

Getting to The Islands of Tahiti

All flights arrive at Faa'a International Airport (Papeete), located near the city of Papeete on the main island of Tahiti. The airport is close and convenient to all the major hotels and resorts on Tahiti. The airport also serves the domestic airline, Air Tahiti, for further service to the other islands and atolls. For schedules and information, check with the airlines, your preferred travel professional, or visit www.airtahiti.pf. We recommend visitors plan international air, inter-island transportation, and airport transfers in advance with your preferred travel professional.

Average flight time to *The Islands of Tahiti*

Paris / Papeete: 20h00

Los Angeles / Papeete: 07h30

Honolulu / Papeete: 05h00

Tokyo / Papeete: 12h00

Noumea / Papeete: 05h00

Rarotonga / Papeete: 03h40

Auckland / Papeete: 05h00

Easter Islands / Papeete: 04h50

Island Hopping

Travel to the neighboring islands is short, convenient and easily arranged. The domestic airline, Air Tahiti, is located at Tahiti Faa'a Airport and offers daily service between the most visited islands. By boat, service varies based on destination: ferries run several times a day between Tahiti and Moorea while cargo schooners sail three times a week for the Society Islands, every two weeks for the Marquesas and the Austral Islands and once a month for Mangareva (Gambier Islands).

Inter-Island Transportation by plane
Air Tahiti operates regularly scheduled flights out of Tahiti over a network of 47 islands and atolls including a 7-minutes shuttle service between Tahiti and Moorea. There is a maximum luggage allowance of 50 lbs (23 kg) for passengers reserved in class Y and 101 lbs (46 kg) for passengers reserved in class Z. Divers are granted a supplementary free luggage allowance of 11 lbs (5 kg) on ATR flights for transport of diving gear upon presentation of supporting documents. No luggage allowance for babies. For further information: www.airtahiti.pf

The Society Islands: Bora Bora, Huahine, Maupiti, Moorea, Raiatea, Taha'a, Tahiti

West Tuamotu: Ahe, Arutua, Fakarava, Manihi, Mataiva, Rangiroa, Takapoto, Takaroa, Tikehau

East Tuamotu Gambier Islands: Hao, Makemo, Mangareva

The Austral Islands: Raivavae, Rimatara, Rurutu, Tubuai

The Marquesas Islands: Hiva Oa, Nuku Hiva, Ua Huka, Ua Pou

Cook Islands: Aitutaki, Rarotonga

Inter-Island Transportation by boat
Although the plane remains the fastest and most commonly used means of transportation in
The Islands of Tahiti, island hopping by boat is also an option. There is ferry service between islands that are not too distant from one another (such as Tahiti and Moorea or Bora Bora and Maupiti) while cargo schooners, more picturesque and sailing to the Leeward Islands, the Tuamotu Islands, the Gambier Islands , the Marquesas and the Austral Islands , offer cabins and occasionally a space on deck.

Among islands in a same archipelago, there are speedboats or small launches that can shuttle you back and forth.

The sea link between the Island of Tahiti and her sister Moorea is one of the most used maritime routes in the world. This transport, daily used by people living in Moorea and working in Tahiti, offers convenient schedules, a comfortable and inexpensive crossing listing between 30-45 minutes (depending on the ferry) with over 10 rotations per day. This crossing offers splendid views of lagoons and coast of Tahiti and Moorea. With luck, you'll see whales during this crossing which give birth in the warm Polynesian waters every year.

There are 2 Ferry companies / shuttle boats which are to Papeete harbor station :

Aremiti

www.aremiti.pf
Aremiti 5 : Rapid catamaran, 30 min. crossing
Aremiti Ferry 2 : Catamaran, 40 min. crossing

Terevau

www.terevau.pf
Rapid catamaran, 30 min. crossing

Airlines

All flights arrive at Faa'a International Airport (PPT), located near the city of Papeete on the main island of Tahiti. The airport is close and convenient to all the major hotels and resorts on Tahiti. The airport also serves the domestic airline, Air Tahiti, for further service to the other islands and atolls. For schedules and information, check with the airlines, your Preferred Travel Professional, or visit www.Tahiti-Tourisme.org. We recommend visitors plan international air, inter-island transportation, and airport transfers in advance with your Preferred Travel Professional.

International Airlines Companies

- Air France

  www.airfrance.com

  Air New-Zealand

  www.airnewzealand.com

- Air Tahiti Nui

  www.airtahitinui.com

- Aircalin

  www.aircalin.com

- Hawaiian Airlines

  www.hawaiianair.com

- Latam Airlines

    www.latam.com

Inter-Island Transportation by air

Regularly scheduled domestic flights

- Air Tahiti

    www.airtahiti.pf

Domestic charter flights

- Air Achipels

    www.air-archipels.com

- Air Tahiti

    (see above)

- Tahiti Air Charter

    (see below)

- S.A.R.L Pol'Air

    www.compagniepolair.com

    Air Gekko

    www.airgekko.com

Service hydravion

- Tahiti Air Charter

    www.tahiti-aircharter.net

Cruise Ships

The greatest sailors in the history of the world first sailed here. Now it's your turn. Follow the ancient Polynesian canoes and European tall ships and chart your own epic South Seas voyage to discover these fabled isles aboard your own yacht.

Navigation

East-west trade winds make for generally easy navigating between the Society Islands and the Marquesas Islands, while a little more caution is required in the Tuamotu Islands, the Gambier Islands and the Austral Islands. One of the Society Islands' strong distinctive features is their location at an amphidromic point, or a tidal system where the tidal range is almost zero. Only the solar tide functions, but it is weak and occurs at the same time every day. The navigation beacons in the lagoons and at the entry of passes through coral reefs in the Society Islands are very efficient. These islands offer many mooring places and nautical facilities for a variety of boats and yachts. A wind known in Tahitian as the *mara'amu* blows between July and September, coming from the south-east and capable of reaching speeds of Force 6-7 (25-30 knots/40-60 kph/25-38 mph).

This causes short and choppy seas, particularly in the channels between islands. Between December and February, a wind from the west can cause strong wind blows.

Coral reef passes

While these passes are wide and passable in all weather conditions in the Society Islands, with the exception of Maupiti in the leeward Islands, it is recommended that they be navigated when conditions are slack in the Tuamotu Islands, where there may be strong currents. In fact, these passes are not very deep and are exposed to strong swells, making them dangerous to navigate, particularly passes exposed to the south when there is a mara'amu, or strong southerly wind.

Moorings

The majority of the Society Islands have deep and sheltered bays. The exterior coral reefs are often bordered with vast expanses of white sand on the lagoon side, are not very deep, and are scattered with coral formations which make heavenly places to drop anchor.

Renting a sailboat with or without a crew (for the more experienced sailors) remains one of the best ways to discover *The Islands of Tahiti*. The almost unlimited number of moorings and the navigational conditions make it a yachter's paradise.

In each island, we suggest you to heed advice in order to select the best place to drop anchor, without disturbing local activities such as fishing in the lagoon, cultured pearl farming...

Papeete Port Authority

The port of Papeete is the only international commercial port in French Polynesia. It is equipped with port facilities that can accommodate commercial and cruise ships as well as pleasure crafts and luxury yachts. Extensive renovations are under way in order to ensure comfortable and secure harbor installations for foreign sailors and the local population alike.

Marinas

In Tahiti, Moorea, Raiatea (the main center for nautical activities) and Bora Bora, several marinas and nautical bases are available for pleasure boaters.

Types of Yacht Experiences

➢ Private Sailing Charter
Crewed sailing catamarans or monohulls sailing multiple islands with flexible itineraries.

➢ Private Motor Yacht Charter
Crewed motorized yachts sailing multiple islands with flexible itineraries.

➤ Sailing Cruise Cabins

Private cabins aboard a sailing catamarans or motorized yacht with fixed itinerary, on an all-incluse package to multiple islands.

➤ Bareboat sailing Charter

Captain of your own catamaran or monohull.

Checklist for the Perfect Sailing Experience:

➤ Trade winds are predictable and weak to moderate most of the year.

➤ Inter-island sailing is short and voyages can include multiple islands and atolls.

➤ Virtually every island and atoll has an 80°F (27°C) neon-blue lagoon.

➤ Lagoons are calm and protected with many anchorages.

➤ Passes are wide, have weaker currents, and feature beacon systems.

➤ Supplies are easily found at island markets, marinas, shops and food stands of fisherman and farmers.

➤ Safety is a part of the islands' ocean culture with a permanent VHF maritime radio channel, daily meteorological reports, emergency services and medical evacuations.

➤ Choices among many expert charter companies.

Cruise Ships and Yacht Charters

M/S Paul Gauguin

www.pgcruises.com

Windstar Cruises

www.windstarcruises.com

Aranui 5

www.aranui.com

Dream Yacht Charter

www.dreamyachtcharter.com

Haumana Cruises

www.haumana-tahiti.com

Tahiti Yacht Charter

www.tahitiyachtcharter.com

Charters Operations Only

The Moorings

www.moorings.com

Sunsail Yacht Charters

www.sunsail.com

Sailing Huahine Voile

www.tahitisailingcharter.com

Ultimate Lady

www.pacificavenues.com

Visas & Entries

Any foreign visitor coming to French Polynesia is required to have a according to the following conditions: In all cases, visitors must hold a valid passport.

1.Stays less or equal to three months (for leisure purposes)

ALL FOREIGNERS are requested to hold a visa to enter French Polynesia, except citizens from:

-An **EU country** (Germany, Austria, Belgium, Bulgaria, Cyprus, Croatia, Denmark, Spain, Estonia, Finland, Greece, Hungary, Ireland, Italy, latvia, lithuania, Luxemburg, Malta, Netherlands, Poland, Portugal, Czech Republic, Rumania, United Kingdom, Slovakia, Slovenia, Sweden);

-Visitors holding a residence permit granted by one of the EU country members or within the Schengen area;

-From the European Economic Area (Iceland, Liechtenstein, Norway);

-From Andorra;

-From Monaco;

-From San Marino;

-From Vatican;

-From Switzerland;

Countries not subject to a visa requirement for short stays as defined per the decree of December 29th, 2011, in relation with documents and visas required for foreigners' entry on the territory of French Polynesia (www.legifrance.gouv.fr):

Antigua-Barbuda	Marshall Islands
Argentina	Mauritius
Australia (including residents of Norfolk)	Mexico
Bahamas	Federated States of Micronesia
Barbados	Nauru
Bolivia	Nicaragua
Brazil	New Zealand (including residents of Tokelau, Niue and Cook Islands)
Brunei	
Canada	Palau
Chile	Panama
South Korea	Paraguay
Costa-Rica	Saint-Christophe-et-Niévès

El-Salvador	Salomon Islands
United States (including residents of American Samoa and Guam)	Seychelles
	Singapore
Guatemala	
	Tonga
Honduras	
	Tuvalu
Israel	
	Uruguay
Japan	
	Venezuela
Kiribati	
	Western Samoa
Malaysia	
Northern Mariana Islands	

Besides, special exemptions may be granted to holders of a diplomatic or governmental and biometrical passport of certain countries. Regarding short stay visas, visitors must hold a return flight ticket.

2.Stays exceeding three months

Should a foreigner wish to stay longer than a period of three months in French Polynesia, the latter should apply for a long stay visa. The only exception will be for EU nationals, the European Economic Area, Switzerland, Monaco and San Marino.

3.Visa requirements

Prior to their arrival in French Polynesia, applicants must contact the Prefecture of their place of residence (if in France) or the nearest embassy or consulate of their place of residence. Any visa requirement fall within the competence of these authorities. Please check the relevant websites to ask for an appointment and obtain the list of required documents to attach to your long stay visa request in French Polynesia. For any additional information in relation to foreigners' entry and stay in French Polynesia, please contact the "Direction de la Règlementation et du Contrôle de la légalité (DRCL)" by email: etrangers@polynesiefrancaise.pref.gouv.fr

Nationals from other countries are submitted to the obtaining of a visa with the embassy of France or the French consulate of their place of residence, including the foreigners holders of a temporary resident's permit (on 1 year in metropolitan France). This visa has to wear the compulsory mention: "valid for the French Polynesia".

Foreigners who have a permanent residence permit for continental France do not have to secure a visa. With the exception of citizens of the European Union and foreigners holding a permanent residence permit for continental France with 10-year validity, foreigners arriving in French Polynesia must be able to show proof a return ticket or, upon arrival, pay a repatriation deposit.

COUNTRIES EXEMPT FROM TRANSIT VISA REQUIREMENTS	
Bahamas	Papua New Guinea
Bermuda	Paraguay
Bolivia	Peru
Colombia	Philippines
Costa Rica	Republic of Marshall Islands
Ecuador	Samoa
Federated States of Micronesia	Solomon Islands
Indonesia	Thailand
Kiribati	Tonga
Nauru	Tuvalu
Palau	Vanuatu
Panama	Venezuela

Tahitian Customs

Customs declarations: upon arrival in French Polynesia, you must declare all goods you are carrying with you and pay the relevant duties and taxes to the Customs Office. However, it is possible to be exempted from paying duties and taxes on goods listed below (purchases or gifts).

Customs formalities

All merchandise must be declared and any relevant duties paid at the Customs Office. Note that when entering or leaving French Polynesia, certain merchandise is subject to special rules. To view the list of such merchandise, visit: www.tahiti-aeroport.pf

The General Directorate for Customs and Indirect Taxation also provides information at the website of the the French Ministry for the Economy, Finance and Industry: www.polynesie-francaise.pref.gouv.fr

Various items and supplies

Tobacco	Quantity
Cigarettes	200 units
Cigarillos	100 units
Cigars	50 units
Pipe tobacco	250g

Alcoholic beverages	Quantity

Still wines	2 litres
Beverages over 22°	2 litres
Beverages 22° or less	2 litres

Other goods (per traveller)

From 15 years old and over	F.CFP 30 000
Under 15 years of age	F.CFP 15 000

People under 18 cannot import duty-free tobacco or alcohol.

For further information, please inquire with French customs services before departure,

Tel.: (689) 40.50.55.50, or go to: www.douane.gouv.fr

Customs Regulations

All items brought in by travelers for their personal use are duty-free, provided they are non-prohibited items and are re-exported out of French Polynesia within six months. All telecommunications and radio equipment require an import license, and certain types of animal life and flora are protected by customs regulations. Strictly prohibited imports include live animals, all plant material, flowers, fruits, and cultured pearls of non-French Polynesian origin. Naturally, any weapons, ammunition, and narcotics are prohibited outright.

Weather

The Islands of Tahiti enjoy a tropical climate; the maximum number of hours of sunshine is close to 3,000 per year in the Tuamotu Islands, one of the highest in the world! The temperature, which is relatively constant, is cooled by the trade winds of the Pacific that blow throughout the year. The average ambient temperature is 78°F/25°C, just as the waters of the lagoons. While further away from the equator, the archipelagos down south, (the Austral Islands and Gambier Islands), enjoy cooler temperatures.

A tropical climate

At Polynesian latitudes, it is summer all year round! However, you can distinguish two main "seasons", dry and rainy. The first lasts from March to November and has temperatures of between
71°F and 80°F/21°C and 27°C; the second, from December to late February, is a little warmer
(between 77°F and 95°F/25°C and 35°C), but also subject to tropical showers, which are like hot showers which rarely last longer than 30 minutes.

The temperature may appear high, but the trade winds from the Pacific blow all the time and refresh the air of the islands beautifully.

Being much further from the Equator, the archipelagos furthest to the south, the Austral and Gambier Islands, have cooler temperatures than the Society and Marquesas Islands. As for the Tuamotu Islands, it enjoys record-breaking sunshine, reaching nearly 3,000 hours of sun per year.

The vegetation is particularly luxuriant during the rainy season, or season of plenty, between the months of November and March. This is also the best time for those who love to sample new tastes as all the tropical fruit are ripe.

Tahiti Currency

How do I exchange money, find ATMs, use credit cards? The local currency is the Pacific franc XPF. For exchange and cash advances, visitors can go to their hotel or cruise ship, Tahiti-Faa'a airport or banks throughout the islands. ATMs are located on the major islands. Major credit cards are accepted in most hotels, shops, and restaurants on the major islands but may not always be accepted at markets, smaller shops and the less visited islands.

Money and exchange facilities

The currency used in *The Islands of Tahiti* is the the Pacific franc (international abbreviation: XPF). An interesting feature of this currency is that its exchange rate with the euro never varies and is set at 100 F.CFP = 0.838 Euros (or 1 Euro = 119.33 F.CFP).

The following are accepted: all legal currencies, international credit cards, travellers' cheques (a commission of approximately 3.5 Euros is charged to exchange these). The international banks on Tahiti and the most visited islands (Banque de Tahiti, Banque de Polynésie, Banque Socredo), have a foreign exchange facility. International hotels also offer this service. Most of the tourist islands have one or more bank agents.

But be aware: Some of the Tuamotu, Gambier and Austral Islands have no exchange facilities. At Tahiti-Fa'a'a airport, two foreign exchange offices (Banque de Polynésie and Banque Socredo) are opened at the arrival and departure times of international flights.

Some practical details

Currency exchange/Buy rates

The following forms of payment are accepted: all legal bank notes, international credit cards, and traveler's checks (an exchange commission is charged on the latter). The international banks with foreign exchange offices on Tahiti and on the most frequently visited islands are the Banque de Tahiti, the Banque de Polynésie and Banque Socredo. International hotels also provide this service but a word of warning: some atolls and islands in the Austral and Gambier group have no banking facilities. At the Tahiti-Faa'a airport, two foreign exchanges offices (Banque Socredo and Tahiti Exchange) are open in conjunction with international departures and arrivals.

Health in Tahiti

The Islands of Tahiti are known for the quality of its health services, thanks to the hospital in Tahiti, equiped with the best of facilities, and its network of clinics, private medical surgeries, dispensaries, infirmaries and first-aid posts on each inhabited island (according to the number of inhabitants), backed up by medical transfers to Tahiti in case of emergency.

On *The Island of Tahiti*, sanitary facilities and health services are available. The cities of Papeete, Taravao (peninsula of Tahiti) and Uturoa (Raiatea) have fully equiped hospitals. Other tourist islands have, at the minimum, a hospital or a clinic.

Tahiti Tourisme reminds travelers that vaccination against yellow fever is <u>obligatory</u> for anyone who has stayed in a endemic country and wishing to visit The Islands of Tahiti.

Yellow fever is a viral disease found in tropical regions of Africa and the Americas. It principally affects humans and monkeys, and is transmitted via the bite of *Aedes* mosquitoes. Since the beginning of 2017, these reports are consistent with the increased yellow fever activity observed in the southern areas of Bahia State, bordering Espirito Santo and Minas Gerais States, and in the areas of Rio de Janeiro and São Paulo States, all sharing the same ecosystem tropical and sub-tropical moist broad leaves forest. Occasionally travellers who visit yellow fever endemic countries may bring the disease to countries free from yellow fever. In order to prevent such importation of the disease, under the *International Health Regulations*, vaccination against yellow fever is mandatory for any person over 9 months who has stayed in an endemic country and wishes to visit *The Islands of Tahiti*. Visitors may be asked for proof of vaccination upon arrival in Tahiti and should be able to provide such documentation to be granted entry.

www.ingramcontent.com/pod-product-compliance
Lightning Source LLC
Chambersburg PA
CBHW021106080526
44587CB00010B/412